Resourcing Mission

Resourcing Mission

Practical Theology for Changing Churches

Helen Cameron

scm press

Published in 2010 by SCM Press
Editorial office
13–17 Long Lane,
London, EC1A 9PN, UK

SCM Press is an imprint of Hymns Ancient and Modern Ltd
(a registered charity)
St Mary's Works, St Mary's Plain,
Norwich, NR3 3BH, UK
www.scm-canterburypress.co.uk

British Library Cataloguing in Publication data

A catalogue record for this book is available
from the British Library

978 0 334 04146 7

Typeset by Regent Typesetting, London
Printed in the UK by
CPI William Clowes Beccles NR34 7TL

Contents

Acknowledgements

I have been actively involved in research into the life of the local church for the last eighteen years. For nine years of that period, I was secretary of the local church I attend. My academic and practical interests have been in constant dialogue – my hope is that this book will contribute to that dialogue for others.

I have been fortunate to have academic colleagues who have shared my interest. The BSA Sociology of Religion Study Group and the British and Irish Association for Practical Theology have been fruitful places to get feedback on my ideas. I have had the pleasure of teaching practitioners on a number of courses, and their questions have challenged my thinking. Particularly valuable has been my involvement in the MA in Consultancy for Ministry and Mission. Over the last decade, students from all traditions have been, often painfully, honest about the challenges they face in working with the local church. Through my research, consultancy, public speaking and individual work consultancy, I have learned from people asking heartfelt questions about their practice.

SCM have been patient publishers. I signed the contract for this book before taking up my present post as Director of the Oxford Centre for Ecclesiology and Practical Theology. The work of setting up the Centre has delayed the book's submission. My thanks to Natalie Watson, Barbara Laing, Hannah Ward and the team at SCM Press.

I am grateful to those who read the case studies in Chapters 3–9. I won't name them, lest the reputation of their denominations is seen to fall upon their shoulders.

On a personal level, I want to thank those who support me in a regular way, to friends and family for their encouragement and to Phil Coull for providing research assistance.

The way in which we make sense of the world is affected by the way in which we see. So finally, I would like to thank John and Kay Thomas for all they have taught me about watching sheepdog trials, and Clive and Marlene Bishop for their perceptions of injustice.

Introduction

I keep in my desk drawer a postcard-sized photograph of a dandelion clock. When words fail me, it acts as a visual reminder of my passion for understanding the life of the local church.

My overwhelming feeling is one of awe, that something so taken for granted can yet possess the reflected beauty of the Creator. But the beauty of the whole is dependent upon the way in which each seed is held together. I am repeatedly inspired by what people coming together in the local church manage to be and to do.

In tension with that feeling of awe is a feeling that, like the dandelion clock, the life of the local church is fragile. For some churches it is very obviously so, as numbers and resources decline. But for all churches, there is a sense that much rests upon the stalwart efforts of a few.

I have to accept that not all adults share my delight in the dandelion clock. Some see my delight as childish or as my inability to call a weed a weed. I cannot ignore those perceptions. Having the courage to be in conversation with people who see things differently is something I hope this book will affirm.

What I try to do in this book is encourage grass-roots theology that helps the reader understand his or her context, ask some challenging questions but without losing the awe of being invited to participate in God's mission to the world.

Structure of the book

This book is based upon two arguments:

1 Churches can think about change theologically using a method called 'the pastoral cycle' that leads from reflection to action.
2 Local churches exist in different cultural forms – the form they take affects the way in which they resource mission.

Chapters 1 and 2 expand these two arguments and form the basis for the rest of the book. Ideally they should be read first. However, if you are someone who resists that kind of bossyness, you are likely to have already skimmed one of the other chapters to judge its usefulness. Now, I hope, you will be open to returning to the first two chapters. Chapters 3–9 can be read in whatever order you wish. There is further guidance on how to use these chapters on pages 42–45.

All books have their limitations. There are a number of things this book doesn't do. It is not a 'how to' book of advice, but the further reading sections in Chapters 3–9 mention some books that do offer practical advice. It is not a systematic ecclesiology offering a blueprint for church life, but rather a practical ecclesiology (Healy, 2000) that discusses the concrete reality of the church and links that to mission. It doesn't offer any prescriptions for mission because I believe that the role that any local church plays in God's mission to the world is best worked out in its own context and in dialogue with its tradition.

Who is this book for?

The book is written for three audiences:

1 those (lay or ordained) engaged in ministry in the local church;

2 those who teach, supervise, mentor and consult with those in local church ministry;

3 those (students and scholars) interested in the academic study of the local church.

The style of the book is tuned to the first audience. I am assuming they are busy people for whom the reading of a whole book is a relative luxury and so books with a clear structure broken into sections have an advantage over flowing prose. I'm assuming some prior theological knowledge but offer suggestions for introductory reading at the ends of Chapters 1 and 2.

For those in the academic audience, Chapter 1 explores my interest in how practical theology can be used in the local church, and Chapter 2 develops my thinking on congregational studies. Where the assertions made in this book are supported by the writing and research of others, I have put the reference in brackets and it can be looked up in the bibliography at the end of the book. Where no such reference is made, the assertion comes from my experience, research and teaching and must be evaluated with that limitation in mind.

This book has been written for Christians of any tradition, but because denominational terms vary, I am using two terms in a generic way.

1 Minister – an ordained or lay person who understands their work for the church (whether paid or unpaid) as ministry.

2 Local church – a worshipping community with a public identity. In some traditions 'the local church' means the diocese, but that is not the meaning here. I have avoided the word 'congregation' because in some traditions that has negative connotations.

How to use this book

As I have written this book, I have envisaged it being discussed and argued about by its readers. I am not expecting all readers to agree with the method of practical theology I propose, or with the models of the local church I offer. It has felt like writing one side of a conversation, and I am grateful to the audiences and students who have answered back when I have tried out these ideas on them. Here are some suggestions as to what the readers' side of the conversation might consist of:

- a personal reflection on ministry;
- a small group in a local church wanting to reflect on resourcing mission – for example, a church council or home group. This may be particularly useful when a local church is contemplating a significant decision, such as the reordering of a building or a new activity;
- a training session for people for ministry, perhaps by setting case studies and questions and encouraging observations of current practice;
- a session in which a mission accompanier or companion helps a local church to reflect upon their practice;
- a session in which a supervisor, work consultant or mentor helps a minister reflect upon their practice.

I would like to suggest there is a way *not* to use this book, and that is in the heat of the moment. A tense church council meeting where there is difficulty agreeing a budget is not the moment to ask whether your opponent has a sufficiently well-developed theology of sin. As the conclusion will argue, finding ways to be kind to one another lies at the heart of changing churches.

How Can Theology be Practical?

There are some social occasions when the appropriate answer to the question, 'What do you do?' is for me to answer, 'Practical theology'. This answer is usually met by a puzzled frown, tinged with the anxiety we display when we are told the punchline to a joke we don't find funny. To the follow-up question, 'What is practical theology?' I usually reply, 'Practical theology is the theological study of Christian practice; it answers the question "How do I know what I really believe until I see what I actually do?"' A surprisingly large number of people are taken aback that theology is interested in such things.

This chapter argues that theology can make a difference in practice. It can make a difference to the aspects of the life of the church which enable it to take part in God's mission. This chapter looks at the relationship between the local church and mission because that relationship underpins the rest of the book. It describes a method of doing practical theology called the pastoral cycle, because that method will be used in Chapters 3–9. In particular, it looks at the challenges of making use of the Bible and Christian doctrine within the pastoral cycle.

Local churches that see mission as the essence of what they are about will be changing in response to their context, the surrounding culture and their dialogue with the Bible and tradition. For such churches, theology is a practical proposition. However, this book is not only written for churches that are already shaped by mission but also for those who are still exploring their essence; for churches who are asking questions about what they do in practice or even wondering if it will rock the boat too much if they raise such questions.

Why the particular issues addressed in Chapters 3–9?

Running your eye down the contents page, I wonder which chapter titles attracted you, and which made you groan. In my experience of teaching ordained and lay ministers, these topics reoccur as ones that occupy a good deal of their time and energy. For some this is done gladly, for others there is the feeling that these topics distract them from the 'real mission'.

A holiday visit to Rievaulx Abbey in North Yorkshire made me wonder if this had always been the case. The site, which is now mostly ruins, has been made accessible to visitors with an interpretation centre, leaflet and headset with a commentary that explores the different parts of the site. From these aids I was able to learn that, throughout its active history, the Abbey had engaged in a range of activities: worshipping God, living by a rule, offering hospitality to pilgrims, caring for the sick, being a centre for learning, engaging in economic activity, inducting the next generation of monks and replicating what they were doing at other places when benefactors offered endowments. What the interpretative material conveyed was that this complex religious, social and economic mission needed resourcing.

The core members of the community were the choir and religious brothers who maintained the pattern of worship. Alongside them were lay brothers who organized and worked in the various aspects of the mission. Their work was supplemented by paid servants who did the manual work and lived on the farms and in the villages. Becoming a brother meant sacrificing family life but offered the guarantee of food and shelter and access to education, which made it attractive to many. The finances of the community were complex. Buildings were usually funded by wealthy benefactors. Sources of income included prayers for the dead, pilgrims' fees and selling the surplus production from the farms. The remaining produce was used to make the community self-sufficient in food, clothing and other commodities. Eventually the Abbey generated substantial wealth. The buildings reflected this growth. Originally simple wooden structures, they were gradually replaced with more and more imposing stone structures. The remaining ruins bear testimony to the awe these buildings must have evoked. A particular feature of the site is the chapter house which is larger than those found on other similar sites. One of the Abbots, Aelred, wanted the lay brothers as well as the religious brothers to be consulted when decisions were made and to listen as chapters from the rule of the community were read aloud. The shared rule and the chapter house framed the governance of the Abbey.

The Abbey was led by an abbot. Abbots of the same order would travel great distances to exchange learning and hold each other to account. As abbots oversaw more wealth and took on secular powers, their emphasis on living by the rule relaxed and their lives became similar to noblemen. The network of abbeys of the same order meant that the offer of an endowment could be quickly responded to and brothers assigned to start a new community, with the expertise and resources of the original community behind them.

Over a long history, the community experienced the risks that affected the rest of the population. Rievaulx was struck by the Black Death and by a disease of sheep that wiped out the wealth they obtained from wool. Finally, a change in state policy by Henry VIII led to the end of the community.

These were the impressions I was left with as a visitor to the site. This was a resourceful community dealing with many practical issues in order to achieve its mission. They seemed all too familiar, even if knowing about the diseases of sheep has slipped from our pastoral agenda today.[1] However, what I felt the interpretation of the site failed to convey was the essence of the community. I learned a lot about what people did and how they organized what they did, but who were they and why were they there? It might have helped to read some quotations from the rule they followed or to know that the Bible was one of the books they studied. But what was the essence of this community?

I now want to look at the question of the essence of the local church and how that relates to mission, before looking at the method of doing theology that will be used from Chapter 3 onwards.

The essence of the local church

The church has a theological identity that logically precedes what it does and how it organizes what it does (Van Gelder, 2000). That theological identity or essence has been described in various ways during the history of the church with the emphasis being placed on certain characteristics over others according to the needs of the age. The earliest definitions of essence are found in the creeds where the church is described as 'one, holy, catholic and apostolic'. At the Reformation, disagreements about the meaning of this essence led to a Protestant emphasis on right order in the preaching of the word and the administration of the sacraments. In the present time, there is a growing consensus that the essence of the church is its participation in God's mission to all creation (Bevans and Schroeder, 2004; Bosch, 1991; van Gelder, 2007).[2]

However, this consensus leaves a lot of room for deciding what it is the church should do and how that doing should be resourced and organized. Let me offer five perspectives which will be developed in the next chapter.

- If the church is the sole agent for God's mission, it is important that it is present in every community and involved in every aspect of that community's life.
- If the church is an exemplary community providing a foretaste of the Kingdom of God but allowing that God may act through other agents, the church can seek partnerships with those other agents, being willing both to give and receive.
- If the church is the people of God dispersed throughout the world throughout the week, the work of the local church may be to equip Christians for mission in the world, heal

them of the wounds they incur and offer a place of retreat from the demands of the world.

- If we live in a post-Christian society that no longer associates the church with a plausible understanding of God, to name God or act in his name requires building relationships of trust and authenticity. The first missional act is to build networks of friendship.

- If we live in a fragmenting and unstable society, the first missional act is to support the nuclear family in its task of nurturing whole human beings as part of God's creation ordinance.

While the theological identity of the church is its primary identity and while what the church does and how it organizes what it does should both flow from what it is . . . in practice, a lot of water has flowed under the bridge in most local churches, and so the common starting point for discussions about mission is usually practice – what we do now. For many local churches a crystal-clear understanding of the relationship between missiology and ecclesiology is not easy to articulate. Churches get bogged down in debate about what they 'ought' to do or be. This 'oughtism' can be restricting rather than liberating. Looking at what a church is actually doing in practice and how they are doing it can be more painful, but facing this reality can in the end be liberating. If what we do suggests this is what we are, then what we could be starts to emerge. Tracking back from practice to essence may be a more fruitful process.

As a practical theologian, I would argue that the essence is identifiable and studying the practice of the local church may be one route to pinning it down. The classic example is the proposal to change the seating arrangements in a church. This often involves fundraising and appraising a range of possible seats – all practical concerns. At some point, someone will ask, 'Why are we doing this?' An exploration of what the church does will be debated. And sometimes someone will also ask, 'Why is this what we do?' So the debate might run as follows: 'We need some new chairs to make the church a more attractive and flexible venue for concerts and so draw a wider cross section of the community into the building than would normally attend worship.' Having established the purpose behind the chairs, a variety of missiological reasons for using the building in this way might be offered:

- It shows our involvement in the cultural life of the community.
- It builds a partnership with local musical groups and helps them achieve their goal of inspiring people through music.
- It offers the church as a place of cultural refreshment from life's demands.
- It enables church members to build relationships with people who don't attend church.
- It enables the local school to put on its concerts and that will attract parents and grandparents into the church where we can make them aware of what we offer for families.

The reality of church decision-making is that the person who keeps asking why is often regarded as a nuisance or obstructive. Hopefully this book will encourage the asking of questions about practice that will lead back to a greater confidence in the missionary essence of the church and a greater fluency in discerning how that mission should be enacted in this place at this time. It may take a leap of faith to see our current practices as bearers of theology, but the promise of practical theology is that this reading of our practices has the potential to transform (Graham, 2002).

What counts as the local church?

In talking about the local church, this book casts its net widely. Below is a map of what this book embraces as 'the local church'. It is important to remember that no map is an exact description of the lie of the land. This map has two dimensions: first, whether the church is an existing historic form of church or whether it is a new form of church; and, second, whether the church is primarily serving the 'churched' (those who habitually attend church at least once a month), the 'dechurched' (those who attend church occasionally – up to six time a year – or who used to attend regularly), or the 'unchurched' (those who have never attended church apart from weddings, funerals and tourism). Tearfund commissioned some research (Ashworth and Farthing, 2007) to try to work out the proportions of the population in these categories. They also asked the 'unchurched' and 'dechurched' if they were open or closed to the idea of attending church regularly. Here are the headline results:

Churched   25% with 15% attend monthly
Dechurched   33% with 5% open to the idea of returning
                to church
Non-churched   33% with 1% open to the idea of going to
                church
Other   9% with 6% of another religion

Map of a mixed economy of mission

	Churched	Dechurched	Unchurched
Existing forms of church	*Parishes and gathered congregations*	*Bridging activities and church plants*	*Life-cycle rituals; chaplaincy; schools*
New forms of church	*Diaspora congregations*	*Emerging church*	*Fresh expressions of church*

Reading this map involves seeing certain forms of church as most likely to engage with 'churched', 'dechurched' or 'unchurched' people. So those who attend church are most likely to be associated with existing forms of church, or, if they are Christians arriving from outside the UK, with diaspora congregations (Chike, 2007). People who are 'dechurched' are often attracted back to church by activities of practical service (Ballard and Husselbee, 2007), by worship at a different time or in a different style, or by the planting of a church in their neighbourhood (Murray, 2008). Some people who are not attracted back to existing forms of church will be attracted by emerging church, which seeks a much closer relationship with contemporary culture (Gibbs and Bolger, 2006).

People who have no experience of the church but who are not hostile to it may come forward for the life-cycle rituals of baptism/dedication, marriage or a family funeral. They will also engage with chaplains as they come across them in institutional or community settings.[3] The Fresh Expressions movement is seeking to stimulate and support forms of church that present the gospel in ways not associated with existing forms of church (Mission and Public Affairs Council, 2004; Nelstrop and Percy, 2008; Croft and Mobsby, 2009).[4]

This map has not sought to lay out a recruitment strategy for the church because mission can be understood in a variety of ways, not all of which include recruiting more members. It has tried to introduce the diversity of local church life and to suggest that some types of church are more likely to engage with some parts of the population. In the next chapter, I will suggest that this has implications for the church's relationship to culture.

Introducing the pastoral cycle

The pastoral cycle is a process for thinking theologically about a particular situation with the aim of finding new and more faithful ways of acting in the future. It has been used widely in both Roman Catholic and Protestant churches and has a track record of being found helpful. It is also a method that has parallels in the world of adult education where the Kolb learning cycle is well known as a representation of how adults learn (Kolb, 1984).

This section briefly introduces this cycle in preparation for Chapters 3–9. The guidance printed before Chapters 3–9 shows how the material in those chapters can be used to support the pastoral cycle. The further reading at the end of this chapter recommends books that explore this and other methods of theological reflection in more detail.

The cycle consists of four stages, each of which builds upon the previous one:

- Experience – what is happening?
- Exploration – why is it happening?
- Reflection – how do we evaluate our experience in dialogue with the Bible and Christian tradition?
- Planning – how will we respond?

The planned response is carried out with this action generating new experiences. A number of writers have pointed out that the cycle is in fact a spiral because having completed the four stages we are not back where we started but in a new place where, having taken action, we can ask again 'What is happening?'

So returning to the example of buying new chairs, mentioned earlier in the chapter, the pastoral cycle might be used by a group looking at the impact of the new chairs after one year.

- Experience – has anything changed as a result of installing new chairs? The views of those whom it was hoped to attract into the building, as well as regular worshippers, would be sought.
- Exploration – why have any changes occurred and what have been their consequences for the church and its community?
- Reflection – how do these changes relate to the original missional intentions at the time the chairs were bought? What influences from the Bible and our tradition can be used to interpret this evaluation? What insights have we gained? Where is God in all this?

- Planning – how will we respond to what we have learned from our reflections?

It has also been pointed out that the cycle/spiral can be used in situations broader that the term 'pastoral' would usually embrace. In this book I am using the pastoral cycle to examine the ways in which the local church resources mission.

Criticisms of the pastoral cycle

Some writers have pointed out the limitations of the pastoral cycle (Wijsen, Henriot et al., 2005). Clare Watkins has argued that the use of the Christian tradition is more than one step in the process of theological reflection. The Christian tradition needs to frame the whole cycle: that is, it influences the experiences we choose to focus on, the way in which we explore them, the way in which we select parts of the tradition and interpret them and the way we decide what future action to take.[5]

Other writers have raised concerns about the relationship between theology and other secular disciplines that are used to explore the experience. Swinton and Mowat (2006) argue that theology has the normative power to 'baptize' the other disciplines so that the theological agenda dominates. Forrester (2008) takes a more dialogical view and argues that theology may receive a critique to its own assumptions and that theological fragments will give insights into our complex world but not necessarily an overarching resolution.

While for ease of communication I will present the pastoral cycle as four stages, my aim is to work with it as a commitment to viewing situations in a multi-dimensional way, combined with an imperative to act. The first dimension is to understand our practice and the effect it has. The second dimension is to explore what affects that practice. The third dimension is to understand the context within which the practice takes place, and the fourth dimension is to know the history and tradition that shape our practice and how we interpret and transmit them. All four dimensions have the common aim of making our practice more faithful to God's mission.

Let me use an analogy to suggest the relationship between the different dimensions. A sheepdog trial can be watched in a number of different ways.[6] The most straightforward is to focus on the interaction between the dog and the sheep. Does the dog successfully guide the sheep around the course, moving them between obstacles at a steady pace and in a straight line? This is the way of viewing sheepdog trials that television programmes tend to adopt, with the shots being mainly of the nose of the dog and the rear of the sheep with the occasional panning shot to see if the sheep are on course. Shepherds find this TV coverage frustrating. They want to watch the way in which the handler works with the dog. What commands does the handler give? Does the dog readily obey? Does the handler misread the behaviour of the sheep and so misdirect the dog? Does the dog have the courage to disobey and follow her reading of the situation? A further challenge in taking part in a sheepdog trial is reading the lie of the land. A keen handler will arrive early before an important trial and walk around the course spotting the dips and bumps in the field that may throw the sheep off line or obscure the dog's view of the sheep. This additional effort can pay real dividends during the competition.

So an experienced spectator is watching the interaction of dog and sheep, the behaviour of the handler in working with the dog and the way in which the handler is reading the field. However, there are some spectators who will add the lens of history to their observations. They will know something about the breeding of many of the dogs taking part and will be looking for characteristics of that dog's parents and grandparents in her performance. They will know something of the track record of the handler, what they have won in the past, the kind of mistakes they make under pressure. Some shepherds will have a complete set of stud books to trace back the ancestry of a dog that interests them. Others draw upon years of experience.

Much of this knowledge is reinforced and developed through informal conversations with other shepherds while watching a trial. Shepherds with this historical level of insight are seen as sources of wisdom when making decisions about purchasing, breeding and training dogs. It is acknowledged that underlying this dimension of knowledge is a commitment to being there, watching attentively, taking part and sharing your knowledge freely in order to gain from the knowledge of others. No one arrives at their first sheepdog trial able to watch in this way. The stages of observing sheep, dog, handler and terrain help build skill in making sense of what is going on.

At its best, the pastoral cycle is more than a series of mechanically followed steps. It is a commitment to a way of seeing that involves participating in oral and written traditions as well as a commitment to reflect upon your practice. At one level this seems blindingly obvious, but it needs stating because we live in a society that is sceptical about the need to immerse yourself in tradition over many years – it wants to cut to the edited highlights and the key tips for success. In some church traditions, the disciplined formation of young people and new adult believers in worship, scripture, tradition and prayer has been set aside. However, studious engagement with the tradition does not remove the need to gain practical wisdom by taking part. But we all have to start somewhere; having a process with steps helps to build confidence and skill.

A final point to make about the pastoral cycle is that although it is bold enough to suggest that theology can arise from our experience, it does not insist that experience is always the starting point. New information about our context can lead us to reframe our experience. The exposition of scripture in a Bible study or sermon can cause a rethinking of carefully made plans. The only way to subvert the pastoral cycle is to refuse to take action and so cut ourselves off from fresh disclosures. Our practices come to life in particular performances, and a performance to which we are committed generates a flow in which we are able to give ourselves fully, uninhibited by the knowledge that each performance will contain imperfections.

The experienced practitioner will know that these imperfections can be grist to the mill of the next cycle of reflection.

Making use of scripture

In reflecting theologically on resourcing mission, I cannot avoid the Bible. My childhood and teenage years were marinated in the Bible. Sunday school, Bible classes, taking scripture exams and listening to sermons were part of my regular diet. I didn't find this dull or restricting, it left me wanting to know more. I decided to study theology at university in an attempt to get the big picture. That was enjoyable, but it seemed to bracket out the church, and I was left to my own devices in making connections between my study and the practices of my church.

In the last decade this situation has been transformed. Textbooks are now being produced that help students understand the art of interpreting the Bible for pastoral practice at the same time as they engage with the historical and critical study of the Bible (Holgate and Starr, 2006). The 'Using the Bible in Pastoral Practice' project has resulted in a series of publications that help ministers make use of the Bible in their day-to-day ministry (Ballard and Holmes, 2005; Oliver, 2006; Pattison, Cooling et al., 2007). The *SCM Studyguide on Theological Reflection* contains a chapter on the use of scripture in theological reflection (Thompson, Pattison et al., 2008, ch. 4). All these sources of advice remind the readers that they should seek to work in a community of interpretation where they test their readings against those of others. This book encourages the local church to see itself as such a community of interpretation.

For those directly involved in the ministry of the local church, the Bible is a resource that is readily to hand, which is already being used in some way and which can provide a focus for debating sensitive issues. Safeguards for the appropriate use of the text must be those that are readily available to those who minister in local churches, for example consulting a one-volume Bible commentary for an overview, consulting a commentary on the particular text being used and then checking against a commentary from a different culture or perspective from my own.[7]

Holgate and Starr (2006, p. 187) quote a World Council of Churches document:

> Just as Scripture constantly looks forward in hope to God's future, the interpreting activity of the Church is also an anticipatory projection of the reality of the signs of God, which is both already present and yet to come. Reading 'the signs of the times', both in the history of the past and in the events of the present, is to be done in the context of the announcement of 'the new things to come'; this orientation to the future is part of the reality of the Church as a hermeneutical community. Therefore the struggle for peace, justice and the integrity of creation, the renewed sense of mission in witness and service, the liturgy in which the Church proclaims and celebrates the promise of God's reign and its coming in the praxis of faith, are all integral parts of the constant interpretative task of the Church. (World Council of Churches Faith and Order, 1998, pp 19–20)

Using the Bible as a shared text has the advantage that it is robust enough to survive our disagreements. If we have honest differences of opinion around the text it may help us to respect honest differences about practice.

Making use of tradition

I have already described how an enjoyment of studying the Bible led me to read theology at university. However, as a teenager, I was also required to study the doctrines of my denomination. This was a different type of 'big picture' which suggested that there was an overall framework of belief that had arisen from

Christian history and was an ongoing focus for debate and truth-seeking. So choosing a degree that contained substantial chunks of history and doctrine seemed a logical choice. Again, at university, there seemed to be a bracketing out of the contemporary church even although the material I was studying had emerged from the life of the historic church. I was left wanting to ask questions about the contemporary church but not sure how to phrase them.

Resources to support the use of doctrine or systematic theology in the process of theological reflection seem less available than those on the Bible. Recent textbooks offer routes into systematic theology for those who have not had previous teaching (Marsh, 2007; Higton, 2008). Richard Clutterbuck (2009) looks at some of the challenges the church faces in teaching doctrine and making use of it in the life of the church. So, for example, doctrine can be seen as divisive or leading to an arid Christianity divorced from emotions. An emphasis on doctrine can be feared as stifling individual freedom of thought or a distraction from action. However, if our reflections on our experience are to be truly theological they need to engage with the core doctrines that frame our tradition. Graham, Walton and Ward (2005), in their first volume on theological reflection, argue that all the major developments in Christian doctrine have arisen from issues of practice in the life of the church. So they propose that doctrine has three crucial roles in the church, roles that shape theological reflection:

> First, theology informs the processes that enable the *formation of character* ... Second, theology assists in building and maintaining the *community of faith* (including determining where the normative boundary of faithful practice might lie, and thus the distinctiveness of the collective identity of Christians). Third, theology enables the relating of the faith-community's own communal identity to the surrounding culture, and the *communication of the faith* to the wider world. (p. 10, italics in original)

In this book my aim is to bring doctrine into the dialogue when reflecting upon the issues the local church faces in resourcing mission. But the challenge is that I cannot anticipate the tradition or sources that the reader and their local church might draw upon. Because of this I am using Duncan Forrester's metaphor of mining for theological fragments, and in Chapters 3–9 propose doctrines that it might be helpful to consider and my reasons for selecting them.[8] My suggestions can be set aside or used as signposts to mine your own tradition for insights that are illuminating. Elaine Graham uses the phrase 'excavation of the sources and norms of Christian practice' to describe practical theology (Graham, 2000: 106), which mirrors Forrester's image of mining for theological fragments that will sharpen our thinking about our practice. There is a tension here between seeing doctrine as a systematic 'big picture' and using it in a more tentative and fragmented way to shed light on our practice.

It is a challenge to discern the essentials of faith in any given context and articulate them in ways that are comprehensible. But without this, practical theology can become a rational analysis reliant on human reasonableness and ethical intention. The representation of major themes in salvation history is essential if the power of the gospel is to be made available to transform practice. However, the focus on practice roots theology in a community of believers and avoids reducing it to individual opinion or sentiment.

Summary

This chapter has sought to make the argument that doing theology (through the pastoral cycle) can make a difference to the local church as it seeks to live out its essence as a participant in God's mission to the world.

This argument has had some important steps that are summarized here:

- Although the theological essence of the church is mission, it is not always easy for churches to articulate their understanding of their role in God's mission.
- Asking questions about practice can be a helpful way of tracking back from how the church is organized, to what it does and then to why it does it.
- These questions are best dealt with in a methodical way and the pastoral cycle is offered as a tried and tested approach.
- However, all methods have their advantages and disadvantages and so the artificiality of doing theology in steps is recognized but seen as helpful in building up a multidimensional perspective.
- Two further challenges were noted: first, using scripture in a way that makes appropriate use of historical scholarship but without avoiding the creative dialogue between experience and text; second, using the doctrinal themes of tradition but without getting sidetracked into a debate that becomes a substitute for action.

Further reading

Ballard, P. and J. Pritchard (2006), *Practical Theology in Action: Christian Thinking in the Service of Church and Society*, second edition, London: SPCK.
Introducing practical theology and the pastoral cycle.
Bevans, S. B. and R. P. Schroeder (2004), *Constants in Context: A Theology of Mission for Today*, Maryknoll NY: Orbis Books.
A text book on mission theology showing its relationship to doctrine.
Clutterbuck, R. (2009), *Handing on Christ: The Gift of Christian Doctrine*, London: Epworth.
A discussion of the challenges in using doctrine in the life of the church.
Graham, E. L., H. Walton et al. (2005), *Theological Reflection: Methods*, London: SCM Press.
Chapter 6 describes the origins and development of the pastoral cycle.
Higton, M. (2008), *SCM Core Text: Christian Doctrine*, London: SCM Press.

An introduction to studying Christian doctrine.

Pattison, S., T. Cooling et al. (2007), *Using the Bible in Christian Ministry: A Workbook*, London: Darton, Longman & Todd.

A workbook guiding reflection on the use of the Bible in ministry.

Thompson, J. with S. Pattison et al. (2008), *SCM Studyguide to Theological Reflection*, London: SCM Press.

An excellent guide for individuals or groups wishing to do theological reflection that assumes no previous experience.

Wijsen, F., P. Henriot et al. (eds) (2005), *The Pastoral Circle Revisited: A Critical Quest for Truth and Transformation*, Maryknoll NY: Orbis Books.

Essays looking at the use of the pastoral cycle in different social and theological contexts. Appendix 1 gives straightforward guidance on undertaking the cycle.

Notes

1 This is not to forget the work done by rural churches during the outbreaks of foot-and-mouth disease and blue tongue.

2 D. J. Bosch, *Transforming Mission: Paradigm Shifts in Theology of Mission*, Maryknoll, NY, Orbis Books, 1991, has been the most influential book in conveying this understanding: 'Mission is thereby seen as a movement from God to the world; the church is viewed as an instrument for that mission ... To participate in mission is to participate in the movement of God's love toward people, since God is a fountain of sending love.'

3 Chaplaincy has been associated with ordained ministers set aside from the local church to work in public institutions such as hospitals, prisons and the armed forces. Increasingly, chaplaincy is occurring in more ad hoc ways with sports teams, shopping centres and old people's homes.

4 Fresh Expressions is a term officially used in the Church of England and Methodist Church to describe groups who are or who are on the way to being church for the unchurched. However, there is a vigorous debate as to whether this is the same as emerging church and another vigorous debate about whether all Fresh Expressions are seeking to connect with the non-churched (Nelstrop and Percy, 2008).

5 These insights have emerged from a research project, *Action Research: Church and Society*; for further information see www.heythrop.ac.uk/index.php/content/view/1003/466

6 For those unaware of sheepdog trials an introduction can be found at: http://www.isds.org.uk/society/handling_trailling/what_is_trial.html

7 In this book I have made use of two one-volume commentaries: A. E. Harvey, *A Companion to the New Testament*, Cambridge, Cambridge University Press, 2004; and T. Adeyemo (ed.), *Africa Bible Commentary: A One-Volume Commentary*, Grand Rapids MI, Zondervan, 2006.

8 In doing this I make use of the one-volume book on the Christian tradition: P. C. Hodgson and R. H. King (eds), *Christian Theology: An Introduction to its Traditions and Tasks*, second edition, London, SPCK, 2008.

2

How are Churches Changing?

Introduction

This chapter sets out the second argument upon which this book is based: the local church cannot escape a relationship with contemporary culture and so it needs to 'read' the cultural signals it sends out, to ensure they are consistent with the essence it wishes to convey.

As Chapters 3–9 will show, these cultural signals are embedded in the everyday practices of the local church and so communicate alongside whatever overt proclamation the church is making. To start with a straightforward example: how is coffee served at the end of the Sunday morning service? Do you pay, and if so is it less than you would at Starbucks? Do you make a donation or is it free? The remaining chapters of this book aim to show that everyday practices like this send out cultural signals and that these signals contain implicit theological messages. In a culturally savvy world people are well equipped to read these messages. Our familiarity with the practices of our local church may have affected our sensitivity as readers (Staub, 2007).

The main part of this chapter introduces five cultural forms that the local church adopts in the UK today and indicates both their history and the way they are read in society.[1] The chapter then loops back to the discussion in Chapter 1 about theological method and mission. After a final summary, there is recommended further reading.

The relationship between gospel and culture

This book uses the term culture in an all-embracing way to include the objects, texts and images that surround us.[2] There are a number of books that help Christians engage with culture (Lynch, 2005; Vanhoozer, Anderson et al., 2007; Ward, 2008). They argue that it is difficult to be involved in mission to a culture we don't understand. Furthermore, it is difficult to discern whether or not we should embrace or censure any particular aspect of culture until we have tried to understand it on its own terms. These books also make it clear that culture does not communicate through factual propositions but rather through signs which need interpreting. What is more, there can be a difference between what an author intends when producing a cultural text, and what the audience receives when they consume that text. Ordinary people are skilled readers of culture, looking for clues to interpretation such as whether the text is part of a particular genre or whether the text builds its credibility by allusions to other texts. So, for example, a design of a jumper formerly associated with middle-aged, middle-class golf players can become the height of street fashion among young people if associated with the right celebrity. Such is the volume of cultural information reaching us that we use short cuts like genre to help us decide what to engage with. So I may use trailers to help me decide what to watch on the television. The mention of the word 'thriller' may attract my interest, but if it is preceded by the word 'psychological' I will lose interest fearing that I may spend valuable time watching something shot in the dark and with no real resolution as to 'who did it'. I have probably missed some excellent programmes but I have probably also saved myself time that I would otherwise have regretted. These rather arbitrary judgements speed up our ability to deal with overwhelming choice. These reading strategies are so embedded into our daily lives that we are scarcely aware of using them.

If the use of genre and allusion apply to our engagement with cultural texts, I want to argue they will also influence the way in which people read local churches. Even where a church consistently seeks to communicate the gospel in propositional terms, it will still be read as a cultural text – a series of linked signs that locate it within a wider culture. As with other texts, the church can be intentional in what it seeks to communicate but it cannot control the way in which it is read.[3] Local churches need to 'read alongside' those who encounter them and then to put that reading alongside their understanding of God's mission and the part their church plays in that mission. Some churches will already be doing this because they have chosen a cultural form deliberately in order to enculturate the gospel into a society that they believe has ceased to understand it. For those who haven't, this book offers encouragement to consider how they are being read.

By definition, a lot of culture is taken for granted which makes it hard to question. But because culture is used to signal differences such as age, gender, economic class, education and ethnicity, it can unwittingly convey attitudes at odds with the essence of the local church. A further reason for taking culture seriously in the study of the local church is that it has assumed a much greater importance in our lives over the last forty years. Some sociologists argue that we create our identity not so much by what we produce as by what we consume (Davie, 2006; Glendinning and Bruce, 2006; Sennett, 2006). The market puts a great deal of effort into allowing us to signal who we are and how we are different from each other by the mass-produced items we consume. The pressure is most acute on children and teenagers who know that the purpose of a trainer is not to keep their foot shod while they run around but to signal to their friends that they are culturally cool. The anguish of the wrong pair of trainers is not the anguish of uncomfortable feet, but the pain of social exclusion. It is tempting to feel that mature Christian adults can rise above the use of physical objects to signal their identity but the disputes in churches over types of music and seating arrangements suggest this may not be so and that cultural objects signal real differences. In fact, the intensity of these debates suggests that we realize how important it is to send out the right signals.

Culture and organizational form

If we accept that the form a text takes will shape our reading of it, then I want to argue that the cultural form an organization takes will shape our response to it. An initial example is the supermarket. The usual organizational form for a supermarket is the bureaucratically structured branch of a large corporation. Although there are no instructions posted outside on how to use it, it evokes a remarkably standard set of behaviours, such as parking as near to the door as possible, collecting a basket or trolley, visiting the aisles in order from the door, queuing at checkouts, and unpacking and repacking goods from the conveyor belt. However, as any surreptitious glance into a neighbouring trolley will tell you, supermarkets resource a wide range of lifestyles and enable people to construct complex identities by exercising taste in what they consume. Many of those choices are a response to cultural clues carefully encoded in the packaging and associated advertising. A pack of fresh podded peas in a cellophane pack may signal a busy professional woman with a dinner party to prepare. A pack of economy frozen peas may signal a busy working-class mother needing to get the kids' tea before she goes out to her part-time evening job. The French sociologist Pierre Bourdieu has argued that social difference is marked by taste (Bourdieu, 1979, 1984).[4] In this case, the physical taste of the peas may be hard to distinguish, but the price and the packaging signal the social and economic differences between the two women. In most towns there are several supermarkets to choose from and they use advertising to differentiate themselves and appeal to different types of shoppers. As the advert for one of them says, 'This is not just food . . .'.

If organizations such as supermarkets, use location, décor, price and packaging to signal taste, they provide the resources for people to make social distinctions. If people are accustomed to reading signals such as this to help them exercise taste, then they are likely to be looking for similar signals in their reading of the local church. For the local church, it is important that the cultural signals it sends out are consistent with its interpretation of the gospel. Churches need to take a reading alongside others to ensure that their cultural signals convey the essence intended (Tanner, 1997, p. 70).[5]

Five cultural forms[6]

I want to argue that most local churches belong to one of five genres or cultural forms, each of which communicates a different set of messages. Chapters 3–9 will explore the implications of these cultural forms for the task of resourcing mission.

Type of church	Cultural form
Parish	Public utility
Gathered congregation	Voluntary association
Small-group church	Book groups and party plan
Third-place church	Secular third places
Magnet church	Parental choice of school

The first two cultural forms, parish and gathered congregations, comprise the majority of local churches because of their historic roots. The other three forms, (small-group church, third-place church and magnet church) are more recent, but act as a useful indicator of attempts to enculturate Christianity into contemporary UK society. I am not saying that the type of church is the same as the cultural form, but that this type of church sends off similar cultural signals to its corresponding cultural form and so can expect a similar response from people attempting to read it.

These five forms cannot be tidily transposed onto denominational distinctions. Some denominations that were once entirely one form have become diverse. Some local churches are hybrids of a historic and a more recent form. This chapter moves on to describe each of the forms.

Parishes as public utilities

It is to Grace Davie that I owe the insight that parish churches are in their cultural form like a public utility.

> Europeans approach their churches not so much as firms but as public utilities. Herein lies the essence of the state church mentality: churches exist (rather like the water or electricity supply) to be made use of when necessary. Such a mentality, moreover, is ill-suited almost by definition to the market, be this financial or cultural. (Davie, 2003, p. 276)

The parish originated in medieval times where it emerged as a subdivision of the ecclesiastical area administered by a minster. The parish conferred two benefits on a geographical area: the services of a priest (to conduct religious worship and officiate at baptisms, weddings and funerals) and a church building. It evolved as both a civic and an ecclesiastical area, but through the population shifts of the Industrial Revolution the boundaries became increasingly less likely to be a co-terminus and less likely to be relevant in the day-to-day lives of residents. However, the parish was always closely linked to the need of the state to be in touch with all its citizens and to tax all its citizens (Pounds, 2000). Following the growth of dissenting churches, church taxes were abolished in 1868, leaving only civic rates and breaking the tie to all property owners (Snell, 2006, p. 418).

The UK is covered by three ecclesiastical parish systems: the Church of England, which took over the boundaries present at the Reformation (and its Anglican equivalents in Ireland, Wales and Scotland); the Roman Catholic Church, which reintroduced its parochial system in 1850; and the established

Church of Scotland. They are often linked with schools which are state funded but have a Christian ethos.

Advocates of the Anglican parish, argue for it as an inclusive form of local church whose territorial nature ensures a presence in every corner of the land and a willingness to serve every resident (Ecclestone, 1988; Bayes and Sledge, 2006). Others would suggest that many Anglican parishes have become gathered congregations, relating more to a particular social group or theological tradition than a geographical locality (Tiller, 1988).

Warner opens up the analogy of public utility:

> The state church (and the quasi-state Roman Catholic Church of southern Europe) retains cultural privileges and may even implicitly claim cultural hegemony: no longer an outright monopoly, but certainly most favoured trading status within the religious economy. A state church functions as a quasi-nationalised religious public utility. As the BBC functions in an era of partial deregulation, a state church operates in the partially deregulated religious market. (2006, pp. 390–1)

What makes a public utility a distinctive form is that it offers complete coverage of the country, it has a legal status which gives it a sole duty to supply a service and what it supplies is regarded as essential. Most utility companies are responsible for maintaining a physical infrastructure (such as pylons, sewers or transmitters) that enables the service to be delivered. There is a temptation to lower costs by failing to maintain and invest in this infrastructure.

The parish as a cultural form has real resonance with the public utility, but that form is unlikely to evoke a response of cultural recognition from anyone under 35 who has probably never paid a bill to a public utility other than (as Warner suggests) buying a TV licence. The parish is more likely to evoke the response made to a private utility with a fee being paid for a service as and when it is used. This makes the fact that the majority of the population no longer regard infant baptism, marriage or a funeral in church as an essential service, a key issue in the maintenance of this cultural form.

Gathered congregations as voluntary associations

My doctoral research made me think about the nature of voluntary associations and the similarities between them and local churches. Using previous research, I assembled a working definition of a voluntary association (Cameron, 2004).

Voluntary associations:

- are formally organized
- have offices filled by established procedures (often elections)
- hold scheduled meetings
- membership is gained by fulfilling specified criteria
- there is some formalized agreement as to who does what
- decisions are made by democratic processes whether representative or participative
- members are expected to pay towards the association, normally by a subscription
- members are expected to contribute their time to the work of the association
- members can only be asked to leave the association if they break its rules
- if paid staff are employed, they support the work of the association, enabling the members to carry out the distinctive tasks for which they associate.

One way in which associations have been classified is to divide them into member-benefit and public-benefit organizations. Some associations exist primarily for the satisfaction of their members, for example a hobby association such as model railways. Other associations exist primarily to provide a service to the public, for example a community association. However, the distinction is often difficult to maintain: self-directed or mutual-benefit behaviour has a way of moving outward; altruistic or public-benefit behaviour has a way of moving inward. Each carries the seeds of the other. For example, does a choir exist to satisfy the musical aspirations of the singers or to entertain the audience?

The Industrial Revolution played an important part in triggering new associations. As people's lives became regulated by factory working hours, so they had shared leisure time in which to organize themselves for social, political or leisure purposes. Churches generated a good number of these associations (Yeo, 1976).

The UK has a long-standing dissenting tradition, which has given rise to a range of congregations some of which have evolved into denominations such as the Religious Society of Friends, the Baptist Union and the Congregational Federation. Methodism is a slightly different case of a society starting within Anglicanism but eventually forming a separate denomination. All the examples referred to have associational polities[7] and gather their congregations from across an area but have no legal obligation to provide religious services to that area. Each polity has subtle variations on the associational definition, with some being representative democracies and some participative democracies, some a federation and the Methodists a Connexion of nested associations.

In the second half of the twentieth century, gathered congregations have suffered a continuing trajectory of decline as have most traditional voluntary associations (Cameron, 2003; Heelas, Woodhead et al., 2005). This includes a decrease not only in numbers, but in member activism, causing a concentration of the work of the association into ever fewer hands (Stacey, 1960; Stacey, Batstone et al., 1975).

Gathered congregations still generate the joining behaviour and activism of the voluntary association but for a much smaller proportion of the population than in the past. On engaging with the 'cultural form' of the voluntary association, people know they are expected to show up, pay up and get involved. As the next three forms will show, it is the last of these three that is becoming problematic in contemporary culture.

Small-group church as book group and party plan

The small group has a long history in the life of the church. Some contemporary advocates of small groups as church (Green, 2004) would see the household churches referred to in the New Testament as examples that validate the small group as a legitimate and perhaps even essential part of church life. The Methodist movement has been recognized as central to the development of small groups in modern times (Clutterbuck, 2009, pp. 144–7; Turner, 2002). Originally a society within the Church of England, Methodists would meet in weekly classes where the gospel was explored and then, once convinced of the need for a holy life, would meet additionally in bands, small groups that focused on personal accountability and mutual encouragement. Another significant renaissance of small groups was associated with Catholic liberation theology in South America from the 1960s where base ecclesial communities were formed by organizers to help groups of poor people understand and resist the oppression they experienced (Boff, 1986; Hebblethwaite, 1993).

In the UK, the Charismatic and Restorationist movements of the 1970s and 1980s popularized small home groups for Bible study and prayer, something that has now spread to most mainstream denominations, although its implementation varies (Wright, 1997; Walker, 2002). In the survey of English Church life undertaken in 2001, 37 per cent of respondents said they belonged to a small group for prayer and Bible study and only 1 per cent said that there was no opportunity in their church to join a small group (Churches Information for Mission, 2001).

A final example of small groups is the cell-church movement that has its roots in Asia. The features of cell church are that the small group is the primary experience of church and that the leader of the cell will be part of a hierarchy of leaders that receives teaching and direction from the minister of the church. All cells are active in seeking new members through their personal networks of family, friends and colleagues. The group will divide into two once it reaches a certain size. Cells meet together for celebrations and to hear teaching, but the cell meeting is the focus for worship, fellowship, witness and service.[8]

In the secular world, small groups are popular for purposes such as book groups and party-plan selling. There is surprisingly little academic literature on either of these given their cultural importance in middle-class and working-class communities respectively.

Long (2003), in her study of women's book groups in Houston, attributes this lack of research to the semi-private nature of the groups and that the overwhelming majority of participants are women. Long's description of the book groups she observed has many resonances with the issues faced by home groups. They tend to be socially homogeneous with a desire to meet people with whom one is at ease but who will also provide stimulating conversation. Groups devise practices of leadership, decision-making, rules of engagement for discussions, hospitality and traditions specific to the group.

The research done on party-plan organizations is also limited. The most detailed descriptions of party plan are found in Storr's (2003) ethnography of the Ann Summers organization, which has some interesting parallels with the literature on cell church, albeit that the groups have very different purposes.[9] The cell equivalent is the unit of party organizers who meet regularly at the home of the unit organizer to discuss their strategies for influencing friends and family to host parties. An area manager will regularly draw together the unit organizers for instruction and encouragement. Unit organizers often provide refreshments for meetings which are held in their homes. Apart from the business, organizers set aside time for 'party organisers to talk amongst themselves, share ideas and simply enjoy each other's company'. (Storr, 2003, p. 9).

The use of small groups in the church is numerically significant. Practice is diverse, with home groups and base ecclesial communities seeming closer to the grass-roots book groups, and cell church seeming closer to the top-down party-plan model. The small group as a cultural form offers the benefits of highly relational and experiential religion in the privacy of the home.

Third-place church as church meeting in secular third places

The term 'third place' was first coined by Ray Oldenburg, a US sociologist who wished to campaign against the regeneration of urban neighbourhoods in a way that eliminated locally owned businesses. He defined the character of third places as follows:

> Third places exist on neutral ground and serve to level their guests to a condition of social equality. Within these places, conversation is the primary activity and the major vehicle for the display and appreciation of human personality and individuality. Third places are taken for granted and most have a low profile. Since the formal institutions of society make stronger claims on the individual, third places are normally open in the off hours, as well as at other times. The character of a third place is determined most of all by its regular clientele and is marked by a playful mood, which contrasts with people's more serious involvement in other spheres. Though a radically different kind of setting from the home, the third place is remarkably similar to a good home in the psychological comfort and support that it extends. (Oldenburg, 1989, p. 42)

In a later book he provides case studies of third places which include coffee shops, cafes, book shops, bars, garden centres and gyms (Oldenburg, 2001).

However, most of the third places available in the UK are not locally owned businesses but chains run by large corporations who have recognized the need for these nodes in people's networks and have created outlets that are classified by academics who study marketing as part of the 'experience economy'. Mikunda (2004) argues that people are seeking commercial outlets that are so 'hot' that they become a destination in themselves and so 'cool' that customers enhance their image by being seen there:

> The successful experience concepts of the present combine the longing for entertainment with true, big feelings, with genuine materials and high-quality design and help with our problems in everyday life, with a quick massage of the soul for stressed-out customers. In a nutshell the experience society has grown up. (Mikunda, 2004, p. 6)

My sense is that the growth of the availability of third places reflects the fact that people's networks are becoming more dispersed and so work and home may not be convenient places to meet. As the workplace has become a more intense place for many people, so the home has become a more private place of retreat. Third places often have flexible furniture so that users can form conversational groupings that are semi-private and demarcate one conversation from another. The focus is on the conversation because all the practicalities of the building and refreshments are delegated to paid staff. Users are glad to pay a premium knowing that there is no risk they will be asked to help with the washing up or made to feel guilty if they leave early. People approach these places knowing that once they have made a payment it is for them to set the agenda.

Over the last ten years there has been a mushrooming of coffee shops, leisure centres, gastro pubs and cafes in institutions (such as art galleries and railway stations) where people can meet informally for their own purposes (such as work, learning, friendship, networking, mentoring and family access). It could be argued that the church and the voluntary sector have a long history of providing third places, whether the church hall, the institute or the scout hut. However, these spaces are now perceived as both public and formal and so not appropriate for meetings that happen at times convenient to the participants rather than convenient to the venue.

I have been able to identify four ways in which the local church has experimented with the third place as a cultural form. First, churches sometimes create temporary third places as a means of drawing people into their building. Coffee mornings and drop-ins are held at advertised times but participants come and go as they please. A second, more formalized version of this, is the meal or refreshments associated with many Christian enquiry courses, such as Alpha, Emmaus or CAFÉ (Hunt, 2004), in which part of the building is temporarily turned into a cafe. However, the purpose of these temporary arrangements is not to become church for the participants but to act as a bridge into Sunday worship or small groups.

In addition to these quasi-third places, some churches have set up permanent third places such as cafes, bookshops or sports facilities (Lings, 2007). My analysis of the examples I have visited and read about is that they can be divided into two groups, those that mimic the market and those that seek to subvert it. This is largely done by the boundaries of price and visual appearance. Some church-run coffee shops compete directly with the chains in the quality of service and refreshments and their visual appearance, and so the prices charged are similar. They are credible places to go because they can be chosen from competitors and may even have an edge by being seen as 'a find', 'a bit different' and offering a more personal service and perhaps ethically sourced goods. Other church-run third places are presented and priced in a way that would encourage you to enter and spend time even if you couldn't afford a purchase and were looking for a chat. Church-run charity shops are a good example, where lengthy browsing is acceptable and the staff can be engaged in conversation. The emphasis is on being cheap and cheerful, with the goods on sale being mostly second-hand.

Finally, there are churches who undertake all or part of their activities in a commercially run third place. There are examples of churches meeting in cafes, pubs, leisure centres and nightclubs.[10] An agreement has been reached with the management who are no doubt happy with the extra business this generates for them. An example is the Sanctus1 Fresh Expression in Manchester:

We run two regular events in the city centre: 'II' is a night of contemporary electronic music and creative media, at a bar in the city centre. It is a place for people who have no relationship with any church to come and meet informally with Sanctus1 . . . We are currently working in partnership with City Centre Management and the Methodist Church to establish a venue called 'Nexus' . . . At weekends, a night cafe staffed by volunteers from Sanctus1 will operate from this space, offering a safe and alternative venue for those enjoying Manchester's night scene . . . Sanctus1 is a fragile, incomplete community. We are learning together about what it means to be church in a transient culture. (Edson, 2006, p. 26)

It is this fourth category that are most committed to enculturating the gospel by using the cultural form of third place as a vehicle to communicate what church is. The permanent third places on church premises often have the potential to develop into church as the case study in Chapter 4 suggests.

Magnet church – church as parental choice

The final cultural form I wish to discuss is that of parental choice of school and the way in which I see this being mirrored in churches that I am calling 'magnet churches'. There is limited research on parental choice as it relates to choosing between schools in the state system and opting out of it. I have yet to find any writing that describes 'magnet churches', but when I name this phenomenon to practitioners they can usually give me examples from their area. However, I will describe some research I undertook in which this concept started to crystallize for me (Cameron, 2003). In this section, I will offer a preliminary description of the magnet church, look at the literature on school choice and then discuss how this might be shaping some churches.

In the study, I looked at the churches in an English market town. I found that most churches were bemoaning the lack of families, but three churches were comprised largely of parents, children and grandparents. The first of these three was a Baptist church with a long track record of youth work that employed a professional youth worker and an assistant pastor whose remit was family ministry. The church drew its members from across the town and surrounding villages. The second was a non-denominational church that hired a college as its Sunday meeting space. It had both paid and unpaid part-time staff doing children's and youth work. It was particularly attractive to people who had moved to the town as a basis for commuting. Its members had a wide variety of previous denominational backgrounds. The final church was much smaller, had its own building but no paid minister or staff and was run by a group of lay leaders who were all parents with school-aged children. A number of them were also school teachers and between them they were creating a particular ethos in which they wanted their children to grow up.

The features these and other magnet churches have in common are middle-class professional or managerial lay leaders with school-aged children, paid or voluntary children's and youth workers, a willingness to focus worship on the needs of families (which were expressed as informality, liveliness and fun), and plenty of parking at their Sunday meeting places. Denominational identity seemed irrelevant, although denominations that are able to offer belonging without formal membership seem to have an advantage. There are some Anglican churches in this category who reinforce their role as magnet churches by being part of the admissions process for desirable church-affiliated state schools.

Turning to the literature on school choice, it is possible to see how the act of choosing has become such a dominant motif in responsible parenting. Until the 1993 Education Act, it was assumed that state-funded schools would be under local authority control and offer a broadly similar education to children irrespective of their family background. It was assumed that children would go to their local school with 'local' being defined by a catchment area (not unlike a parish boundary).

However, the introduction of the national curriculum followed by testing at ages 7, 11, 14 and 16 and the publishing of results in league tables made it evident that not all schools were the same and that those in middle-class areas usually out performed those in working-class areas. This gradually had an impact on the property market, with house prices rising in proximity to favoured schools.

A greater variety of secondary schools was introduced successively by Conservative and Labour Governments assuming that this would generate competition between schools that would improve performance. The outcome of this process is that in some parts of the country there are now favoured schools that are in effect choosing parents rather than the other way round.[11]

Moser (2006), in her study of parental choice in rural primary schools, identifies three types of school as important to three groups of parents, the right school, a good school and a local school. Working-class parents prioritize local as the most important criterion. Middle-class professional families look for the right school for their child, assessing the size, ethos and pedagogical approach of the school and seeking a fit with the temperament and abilities of their child. Middle-class managerial parents are looking for a good school and consulting school leagues tables and inspection reports as a basis for that evaluation. If the right or good schools happen to be local then that is a bonus, but there is a willingness to transport children, especially when families are incomers to rural life and see commuting as an accepted part of their lifestyle.

It is possible to make some tentative connections with my earlier data. Churches in the case study town were finding that being local was insufficient to attract middle-class families. My argument is that middle-class parents may be increasingly approaching their choice of church in a similar manner to their choice of school. This makes magnet churches like marketized public services whose performance is judged and where professionals are employed to maintain quality. Switching of church is related to performance and ethos rather than locality and tradition.

As you have read about these five cultural forms, you may have immediately identified one which is a reasonable fit for your church, or you may feel you are operating a hybrid of more than one form, or that nothing quite fits. The purpose of the following chapters is to discuss how mission can be resourced while all the time bearing in mind that the way in which this is done will send out cultural signals that will be read and interpreted.

To compare churches with secular institutions may seem irreverent or to misunderstand the nature of church as holy and different. However, I want to emphasize that the church does have essential qualities but, because these are wrapped in culture, it may be worth making comparisons that disrupt our thinking. The church is not a passive victim of culture but can scrutinize itself and, if it wishes, change things.

The local church and mission revisited

This chapter has suggested that there is a relationship between the local church and culture; that people will make cultural readings of local churches which may or may not be at odds with the intentional messages the church wishes to convey about its essence. It has also been suggested that some churches are intentionally adopting cultural forms that they feel enable them to enculturate the gospel in a way that makes it easier to read in a post-Christian and plural society. This process of reading from the church to culture and from culture to the church underpins the remaining chapters in this book. But before moving on, I wish to offer an initial reading of each cultural form as it relates to the role of the local church in God's mission to the world.

Parishes as public utilities

This cultural form could be seen as an enculturation of the gospel whereby the local church offers an incarnational presence. The missiological intention is to demonstrate God's concern for all humanity by being present in every neighbourhood and feeling an obligation to every resident.

Gathered congregations as voluntary associations

This cultural form enculturates the gospel as a fellowship of the Holy Spirit in which together all believers exercise a priestly ministry to their neighbours. The missiological intention is to offer an alternative society that is a foretaste of the Kingdom of God and provides a solidarity with which to withstand the pressure of culture to conform.

Small-group church as book group and party plan

This cultural form enculturates the gospel in small groups of disciples who seek to learn the way for their lives. The missiological intention is to offer a taste of Jesus' table fellowship and intimacy as a bulwark against an anonymous world.

Third-place church as church meeting in secular third places

This cultural form enculturates the gospel by presenting Christ as friend of all and a companion who is met regularly on life's journey. The missiological intention is to build authentic relationships as the foundation upon which any communication of the gospel, in word or deed, can take place.

Magnet church – church as parental choice

This cultural form enculturates the gospel by creating safe spaces in which children, young people and families can experience the Christian way. Its missiological intention is to value the vocation of parenthood and see it as crucial in building a healthy society.

Summary

This chapter has introduced the idea of cultural form. It has argued that there is an inescapable relationship between gospel and culture and that just like any other social activity, the church will be read as sending out cultural signals. Five cultural forms have been described, two of which have historic roots in the UK, with the remaining three being evident in the way churches are changing. A final section has explored the way in which the five forms might relate to mission.

Further reading

Graham, E. L., H. Walton, F. Ward. (2005), *Theological Reflection: Methods*, London: SCM Press.
See Chapter 7 for a discussion of local theologies that reflect the context in which they are undertaken.
Marsh, C. (2007), *Theology Goes to the Movies*, Oxford: Oxford University Press.
An introduction to Christian theology using movies as case studies.
Lynch, G. (2005), *Understanding Theology and Popular Culture*, Oxford: Blackwell Publishing.
A detailed guide to reading popular culture in a theological way.
Schreiter, R. J. (1985), *Constructing Local Theologies*, Maryknoll, NY: Orbis Books.
A clear guide to doing theology in a local context.
Vanhoozer, K. J., C. A. Anderson, et al. (eds) (2007), *Everyday Theology: How to Read Cultural Texts and Interpret Trends*, Grand Rapids MI: Baker Academic.
A strategy for reading cultural texts with some worked examples from popular culture.

Notes

1 There are other authors who have proposed ways of classifying local churches. The most notable UK example is P. Heelas, L. Woodhead et al., *The Spiritual Revolution: Why Religion is Giving Way to Spirituality*, Oxford, Blackwell Publishing, 2005. And an interesting American example is P. E. Becker, *Congregations in Conflict: Cultural Models of Local Religious Life*, Cambridge, Cambridge University Press, 1999.

2 See K. Tanner, *Theories of Culture: A New Agenda for Theology*, Minneapolis MN, Fortress Press, 1997. 'Incorporating within its range of associations the notions of context, community, convention and norm, "culture" has broken through the disciplinary boundaries of anthropology as one narrowly defined academic field' (p. ix).

3 Missiology uses the term 'enculturation' to describe both the process by which this happens and the result. Some writers also use the term 'contextualization'.

4 For a helpful summary of Bourdieu's thinking on this matter, see Chapter 10 of P. Ward, *Participation and Mediation: A Practical Theology for the Liquid Church*, London, SCM Press, 2008.

5 'Christian theology has to do . . . with the meaning dimensions of Christian practices, the theological aspect of all socially significant Christian action. Christian theology in this primary sense would, accordingly, be found embedded in such matters as the way altar and pews are arranged. Their placement usually has a meaning, a theological aspect, in that it embodies a sense of the difference between minister and laity, and between God and human beings.' Tanner, *Theories of Culture*, p. 70.

6 The idea of cultural form is related to earlier research I have done on organizational form and how it affects learners' response to different types of learning institutions. The definition of organizational form developed in that research was:

Organizational form can be defined as the legal ownership and constitution under which an organization operates. It affects:
• the way in which work is co-coordinated and managed,
• the way in which governance structures and processes render an account to stakeholders,
• the ways in which the organization can secure resources,
• the way in which the assets of the organization are protected and managed,
• the way in which the organization can allocate its resources to pursue its mission,

- the ways in which the organization can establish its legitimacy in the eyes of its users.

H. Cameron and M. Marashi, *Form or Substance in the Learning and Skills Sector: Does Organisational Form Affect Learning Outcomes?* London, Learning and Skills Development Agency, 2004, p. 3.

7 Polity – the particular form of government adopted by a denomination that expresses its understanding of how the will of God is discerned by believers.

8 This is a more top-down approach to small groups and Harvey (2003) likens it to rationalized control akin to the McDonaldization phenomenon identified by Drane (2000).

9 Party-plan organizations sell less controversial products such as make-up, clothing, children's books and kitchen ware.

10 There are now para-church organizations providing materials to support such ventures: see, for example, www.lyfe.org.uk. See the following account of nightclubs as a setting for church: J. Oliver, *Night Vision: Mission to the Club Culture*, Norwich, Canterbury Press, 2009.

11 Reay (2004) evaluates this change negatively: 'The growing policy focus on parents as educational consumers encourages and exacerbates the deployment of middle-class cultural capital in ways which lead to increasing social segregation between schools and pupils' (p. 80).

Guide to Chapters 3–9

Chapters 3–9 are designed to help the reader (whether alone or in a group) work through the pastoral cycle in relation to their experience in their local church. So, for example, Chapter 4 might be used by a church treasurer wanting to think about the way in which money is used in their local church prior to discussions about major changes in the budget. Chapter 8 might be used by a church council wanting to explore whether or not to form a ministry team.

This guide suggests how each section of the chapter might be used.

Experience

Each chapter starts with a made-up case study that illustrates the issue under discussion. These case studies also between them illustrate the five cultural forms of church described in Chapter 2 (see Appendix A). The case studies can be used in two ways: first, when the book is being used for teaching and the group of students do not have experience of one particular church that they share; second, when a minister or group in a local church is preparing to discuss an important or controversial topic and it is helpful to rehearse the discussion using a case study.

For many users of this book there will be a specific experience from their local church that they wish to reflect upon, and so the case study can be set aside. However, it is important not to assume that everyone in a local church views an experience in the same way. This step in the pastoral cycle is about gathering the stories and descriptions from a number of perspectives, finding out what people feel about the experience and whether they have shared or different views about what happened. At this stage people may be able to say how their experience and feelings affected their actions.

In undertaking the pastoral cycle it is important to be aware of whose experience is being explored and who gets to take part in the conversation. Before embarking on the process it is worth discussing how any recommendations for action will be translated into decisions.

Exploration

All experience takes place in a context and the life of the local church takes place within a cultural, economic, political and technological context that is changing. This section explores that context and suggests ways in which it may be affecting the life of the local church. This material can be debated to see if it is relevant to the experiences described. Other factors may become apparent. This discussion may highlight the need to gather further information before the next stage is undertaken. As this information is sifted the implications for the local church need to be noted.

Resources for reflection

Once the experience has been described and explored, it is possible to reflect upon it in dialogue with the Christian tradition. Local churches have different practices in interpreting tradition and so what is offered here is what I called in Chapter 1 'theological fragments', which I hope will trigger reflection on the topic of the chapter. The interpretations offered are mine, although I explain what sources I have used to inform my interpretation.

Local churches exist within a tradition (some more consciously than others), and that tradition may well suggest resources or interpretations that are helpful at this stage of the cycle. The ideas and questions that have arisen in the first two stages may trigger further ideas for resources to be followed up. This stage of the process needs time, both to interpret the chosen resources and to allow them to resonate with experience and suggest new insights. New insights may be met with recognition or they may need to be discussed and weighed to discern their value.

Planning for practice

It is not possible for me, as an author disconnected from your context, to suggest what plans are appropriate for your future practice. What I aim to do in this section is to spell out my understanding of the implications of the chapter topic for the five cultural forms of church described in Chapter 2. I argue that it is in these details of church life that local churches disclose their cultural form. However, your readings of culture may differ from mine and you may identify different implications for your church. It will be important to compare your cultural readings with those of 'outsiders' who lack your familiarity with the church.

This section of the chapter will also suggest exercises you can undertake to inform your planning. These exercises can also be undertaken at the exploration stage.

Views may differ as to whether the appropriate response to new insights should be wholesale reform or incremental change. Whatever changes are made, it is an implication of the pastoral cycle approach that a commitment is made to reflecting on the experience of changes once they have been implemented for a period. For most groups, the confidence to be both self-critical and self-affirming grows as the cycle becomes more familiar.

Further reading

Each chapter ends with suggestions for further reading that can supplement the exploration of your experience.

3

Time

Introduction and purpose

The purpose of this chapter is to look at the resource that underpins all others in the life of the local church, that is, time. The way in which time is experienced and structured has changed substantially over the last thirty years and this has affected the paid and unpaid time given to church work. I will argue that each cultural form of church has its own way of structuring roles and this affects the way in which people contribute time.

The chapter starts with a case study, explores the context of the use of time in contemporary culture, and then offers two theological fragments for reflection. Suggestions are made as to how each form of church can plan for practice. Finally, further reading is recommended.

Experience

All Saints Parish Church

All Saints is located in a village just outside the boundaries of a National Park. The church building is small, well kept, set in a mown churchyard. It attracts some visitors but nothing like the number in neighbouring parishes within the National Park. Over the last twenty years the village has attracted newly retired couples from the nearest big city who have bought and renovated former farm cottages. The city is just too far away to commute but still close enough to visit family and friends, the theatre and the airport.

Mary was one of the first to move into the village. She and her husband had taken early retirement as schoolteachers and wanted to live their dream of village life. It had seemed natural to Mary to continue her involvement in the church and she had become PCC secretary within a few years of their arrival. The involvement had sustained her when her husband died in his early 70s. Now she has had her eightieth birthday and can no longer drive, and so has finally accepted her son's suggestion that she move back to the city to be near him.

She reflects upon how she will break the news to the priest and the rest of the PCC. Over the seventeen years she has done the job she feels people have become less committed to the church. She worries that she is letting the priest down by moving away. One of the churchwardens pays for his gardener to mow the churchyard; another PCC member pays her cleaner to keep the inside of the church clean. The teenage children of the local farmer are paid pocket money to lock and unlock the church and turn the heating on in winter. Even the flower-arranging rota has collapsed, so the gardener keeps up a supply of house plants. The trouble is that it is mainly incomers who attend the church and they are all so busy. Some are on standby to care for grandchildren in school holidays or have to make regular visits to their own elderly parents. They take holidays throughout the year, often taking advantage of last-minute bargains. She knows that the PCC treasurer still does some paid work to supplement his pension. The priest has six other parishes under his care, and she knows that he relies upon her to keep things ticking over and to let him know when someone needs visiting.

Mary keeps on putting off her announcement, but it is the night of the PCC meeting, and she knows she must say something. As she fears, her announcement is greeted with a stunned silence. The priest asks for suggestions as to who might replace her. People start to explain why such a regular commitment would be difficult for them. Then one member has a bright idea, turning to the priest he says, 'We pay our share towards your stipend, you are the only person being paid to attend this meeting, perhaps you could take it on.'

Exploration

In the life of the local church the word 'commitment' is usually hovering in the wings in any discussion about who gives what time for which purpose. Church members of Mary's generation have often lived lives of regularity and discipline, much like those of a school, and so have set aside time on a weekly basis to undertake the work of the church on a voluntary basis. Now that notion of membership seems to be crumbling, not only in church life but in other types of voluntary association.

This section explores ten changes that have both decreased and fragmented the time people have available for voluntary action.[1] Some of the changes made by churches in response to this are discussed. Finally, it looks at how giving time to the life of the church can be surrounded by poorly articulated expectations.

The most significant factor affecting the time available for unpaid church work is the increasing participation of women in paid work. This has not been matched by a corresponding decrease in their domestic and caring responsibilities and so some women see themselves as doing a 'double shift' of paid work outside the home followed by unpaid work inside the home (Hansen and Joshi, 2007, ch. 9). The leisure time they have may be spent multi-tasking, juggling childcare and household tasks with 'time off' (Bryson, 2007). This change also affects the availability of men and children for church activities, as women are unavailable for tasks, such as preparing meals, that free up the time of other family members.

As people enter retirement, it is often with the expectation that they will have more time. For an increasing number this is the point at which the 'care sandwich' takes over. There are expectations both that they will help adult daughters in paid employment by providing free childcare and that they will offer informal or even personal care for older relatives. It is not surprising that people in this position do not want to be tied down to 'unpaid jobs' in the leisure time that is left.

The UK has a culture of long working hours for those in full-time employment, with many exceeding the European Directive limiting working hours to 48 a week (Burke and Cooper, 2008). Fear of redundancy can lead to 'presenteeism', spending long hours at work to demonstrate commitment. For those working long hours (and this includes people like school-teachers who in the past would have had standard working days), leisure time becomes precious. The aim is to spend it doing something that is recreation rather than something that feels like more work.

At the other end of the spectrum are people whose lives are a complex juggling of work and personal life. Agency work-ing, split shifts, short-term contracts, and self-employment can lead to irregular patterns of work that make regular patterns of social life difficult to maintain.

For adults of working age not in employment, what they can do with their time is affected by the benefits they are receiv-ing and the conditions upon which those benefits are awarded. There may be a reticence in undertaking regular voluntary commitments if these are perceived to reduce availability for employment or call in to question the seriousness of health problems.

There are now significant numbers of children whose lives are split between two locations. Which parent they are with affects what they can do, and so participation in weekly activities especially at weekends can be impractical. Parents, grandparents, aunts and uncles can all be involved in the arrangements that shuttle children between one home and another. For the adults involved, their time without the chil-dren is 'free time'.

The UK has one of the highest levels of home ownership in Europe. Owning a home is seen as a major asset securing old age. Investment is made in homes through gardening and DIY.

It is now more difficult for children to change school. These factors mean that people often extend the time they spend commuting rather than move house when they get a new job. Commuting time usually erodes leisure time rather than work time. Evenings become shorter and the weekends a respite from the discipline of early rising.

Those entering retirement at the moment are keenly aware that the combination of their house and pension may not provide sufficient resources for their retirement. The state pension age for women is in the process of increasing to 65 and there are pressures on employers to allow people to stay on beyond 65 if they so wish. In addition to greater insecurity about their own finances, this may be the time when parents are seeking to help their adult children get a foot on the property ladder. All this points to a much greater involvement in paid work of those in their 60s and early 70s, with a consequent reduction in the 'new activities' that retirement might otherwise have made possible.

The preciousness of leisure time to many adults has not gone unnoticed by the market. The increase in eating meals outside the home relieves the time spent shopping for and preparing food. The range and sophistication of entertainment available for consumption at home continues to grow. The larger voluntary organizations market their fundraising opportunities as 'fun runs' or 'experiences' rather than invite people to knock on doors or rattle collecting tins.

Technology has increased the possibility of spontaneity. Informal social gatherings can be arranged in minutes over the Internet and last-minute bargains booked. Being free to be spontaneous is 'cool'. Having to be somewhere reliably on a weekly basis is seen by many as a bind.

It is not possible to calculate precisely the impact of these different factors on the willingness of people to give time for the work of the church. However, it would be possible to look at which factors have affected members of your church and to identify those that have grown in significance in recent years. It would also be prudent to identify who gives most unpaid time to the work of the church and what enables them to be so generous. If the five people who give the most time left at once, what impact would it have? In the research done on sports associations, it is recognized that most sports clubs are unduly dependent upon the effort of a few stalwarts (Nichols, 2006).

The factors I have described affect many parts of the voluntary sector. There have been two main responses to a reduction in availability for regular voluntary work, both of which are also evident in church life. The first response is to pay someone to co-ordinate the unpaid efforts of others. This co-ordinator takes care of the rotas, the paperwork, any red tape and the consequences of people dropping out at the last minute. This leaves the voluntary participants free to enjoy doing whatever it is they have volunteered to do. In church life there has been a growing trend to employ people to do administrative work, to co-ordinate pastoral care, to plan and direct volunteers in the provision of children's work, youth work and social action. These posts are often not very well paid and the skill they require in co-ordinating the voluntary efforts of others is often underestimated. However, they drastically reduce the need for stalwarts who will take their unpaid church 'job' as seriously as they would paid employment. In fact the boundaries for a paid church worker can sometimes be clearer in terms of what is and isn't work and when they are off duty. For a stalwart, there is no trip to the supermarket that can't be interrupted by an earnest discussion of a rota with a fellow church member.

A second response is to formalize the management of volunteer time. Clearer specifications of the work to be done are produced, time is spent matching the skills of the volunteer to the right opportunity, and then the satisfaction of the volunteer with the task is monitored. Morisy (2004) advocates a much less managerial approach for churches, talking of the vocational domain, a journey in which people recognize a much deeper sense of purpose and personal story, which they are willing to align with the work of the church. This approach might focus on welcoming and befriending people, discerning with them their vocation and talents and then journeying with them as they develop through the work they do.

The two responses I have described have the advantage of being intentional. A substantial problem with giving time in church life is the many unspoken assumptions that can surround it. I was alerted to this through the work of the sociologist Fichter (1953), who suggested there were four different ways of being a Roman Catholic: nuclear, with involvement in the work of the parish; modal, with weekly Mass attendance; marginal, with attendance at major festivals; and dormant, with no contact other than baptisms, weddings and funerals.[2] Reflecting on these definitions, I realized that the threshold between one category and another would vary from church to church. What are the expectations of a modal attender in your church? What would you need to do to demonstrate your membership of the nucleus? At what point would your participation be considered so dormant that the church ceased to maintain some sort of contact with you? These thresholds are learned by participation, and for those seeking greater involvement they offer steps to more intensive participation. For those worried about too much being expected of them, they can act as electric fences, helping people keep their distance. It is known for people to move from smaller to larger churches where the expectations of modal members are less onerous. A church that is short of time tends to communicate the fact quite powerfully through noticeboards, newsletters, announcement sheets and even exhortations during worship. Intended as invitations, they can also act as 'electric fences', keeping people on the margins of church life for fear of expectations they cannot match.

Resources for reflection

This section offers two theological fragments designed to stimulate discussion about the use of time in church.

Bible

Feeding of the five thousand (John 6.1–14)

Jesus challenges the disciples to work with the resources they have in the immediate situation. They produce a boy with five loaves and two fish. When I was a child, it was impressed on me by Sunday school teachers that even though I was a child, if I gave generously, it could be blessed and used to help others. It was a pattern of commitment I recognized in the adults around me who were unstinting in their service of the church. Lifts were given, meals shared and babysitting offered to make it possible for people to be in the right place at the right time for the work of the church. Thirty years later, my experience as a church secretary was very different. Tasks, such as Sunday school teaching, which had once been someone's job, were now organized by rotas. If there was work to be done, then participation needed to be negotiated around other commitments to work and family life. This experience redirected my interest in this story to the gathering of the fragments of bread after the meal was over. It felt as if I was trying to make sense of the fragments of time left over from people's busy lives.

The following reflections occurred to me. There are still people who can give generously of their time, but they are often people (like the boy) who are easily overlooked. Burridge (1998) emphasizes that the boy's meal of barley loaves and dried fish was the diet of the poor. So it was a basic as well as a small offering that was multiplied.

There is a need for families to earn their bread and then sit and eat it together. This is a need which it is good to satisfy and it is important to be aware when church life is encroaching upon it. The fragments are already blessed and so worth gathering. Their brokenness does not diminish their value. As A. E. Harvey (2004, p. 320) suggests, it is the scale of what is in the baskets compared with what was given initially that forms the sign of the miracle.

It may be that those who hand in fragments of time are dependent upon those able to give more extensively of their time. How can this be done in mutual appreciation rather than mutual resentment?

Doctrine

Eschatology – the doctrine of time

For a number of years, I taught a module on the management of change to a group of public and voluntary sector managers. As an opening exercise I invited them to place three dots on a sheet of paper, label them 'past', 'present' and 'future', and then with arrows indicate how they understood each to relate to the others. This exercise often provoked discussions about how the teaching of management invariably ignored history and how as managers they often felt pressurized into portraying an unrealistically idealized vision of the future.

Eschatology is the source of sustained Christian reflection upon the nature of time. It draws upon biblical narratives that depict Jesus as inaugurating a new age (Luke 4.16–30) that supersedes the present age, a theme already present in the apocalyptic books of the Old Testament. Carl E. Braaten (in Hodgson and King, 2008, ch. 12) explores four different ways in which Christians understand the relationship between these two ages.

The first understanding sees this world as a preparation for a world yet to come. We are being made 'fit for heaven'.[3] An analogy might be rehearsal time for a better performance. The second understanding sees this world as existing in parallel with the world to come. We can participate in the worship of heaven now when we worship on earth. The third understanding sees the world to come having decisively broken into the present world, through Jesus' inauguration of the Kingdom of God. Participation in this new age is an ever-present possibility for those with eyes to recognize it. A fourth understanding sees the world to come as about to break in on the present world and bring about revolutionary change. There is an impatient focus on the future with its promise of justice and freedom. Different parts of the Christian tradition place different emphases on these understandings and they may shape the way in which time given to the work of the church is viewed.

Time is also a reminder of our limitations as creatures. But the fact that God entered history in the person of Jesus as part of the story of salvation can give us a sense of his trust in humans as co-creators. Our chronologically driven culture can rob us of perspectives on time that the study of eschatology might restore. Worship can reconnect us to a timeline beyond our pragmatic concerns, offering us a broader horizon and different perspective.

Planning for practice

Returning to the five cultural forms of church, this section suggests that each has its own logic when it comes to the shaping of roles through which people can contribute time. The section finishes with two exercises that might provide the basis for further discussion.

Parish

If the analogy of public utility is used for the parish, then the priest is the officer who links the local to the wider national structure and so has the authority to design and delegate work. There may be other officers but their role is defined in relation to the priest. The giving of time is often described as 'helping' the priest and gains some of its significance and reward from its auxiliary nature. Those who help are usually those who appreciate the spiritual significance of the priest's work. However, there may also be people who wish to have an association distanced from belief and so join a 'Friends of the Church', raising funds for the building. They recognize that the building is an 'externality' whose upkeep reflects upon the whole community.[4] This form of church can often rely upon the priest to be the main person who co-ordinates the help people offer.

Gathered congregation

If the analogy of the voluntary association is used for the gathered congregation, there will be a defined membership, most of whom attend worship regularly. Overt membership criteria will usually include a declaration of belief, but there are also likely to be expectations that time will be given regularly. The giving of substantial amounts of time is usually seen as a signal of commitment and the church usually leans on the efforts of these stalwarts in co-ordinating the efforts of others. There are likely to be elected lay officers and, even if elections are uncontested, the authority of office includes that of assigning work to members. However, where members are seeking to minimize their involvement this authority may in fact be exercised through negotiation and persuasion. A smaller number of stalwarts may end up supporting a larger periphery of members, risking burn out. In some denominations this is coinciding with reducing numbers of ordained paid ministers.

Small-group church

In small-group church, the key mobilizers are the leaders of the small groups. This role is usually well defined, with expectations both from those with oversight of the whole church and from the group members themselves. The small-group leader usually takes the brunt of practical organization away from the group members so they can focus their time on participation and the satisfaction that brings. Some churches recognize the load this places on small-group leaders and employ staff to give them administrative support. Those leaders with oversight see the recruitment, training and support of small-group leaders as their primary task, because they have delegated day-to-day pastoral care and mission to small groups. Small-group leaders are usually appointed rather than elected and so their style of working is usually to mobilize and enthuse members rather than delegate work.

Third-place church

Third place church has two different types of work that operate in parallel. The primary work is done by paid or unpaid leaders who animate participation and interaction between those attracted to the third place. This may consist both of drawing together teams who will create events for the participants and also developing relationships between participants. The secondary work is that of running the venue in which the participants meet. This work is often paid for because the venue is run by a separate organization, such as a club, pub or cafe. Some third-place churches own and run their own premises and risk the danger of that work deflecting leaders from their primary task. In either case, the aim is for the venue to become a stage on which the life of the participants becomes a shared story. The participants may scarcely be aware that they are giving time through their participation. The aim of the leaders is to create an ethos of well-organized informality.

Magnet church

Magnet churches are professionally run. Their substantial involvement with children and teenagers means that key leaders have to 'know what they are doing'. Member giving supports sufficient paid staff to ensure this is the case. However, it is also possible for members with professional skills, such as teachers, accountants and lawyers, to do pro bono work. Structures and accountabilities are usually clear with those who wish to give time being allocated volunteer opportunities that are supervised. The equation between time and money is usually well understood, with parents seeing church as among the 'paid-for' activities their children undertake alongside music, sport and performing arts. There tends to be an emphasis on planning, preparation, training and evaluation so that the best use is made of time given. School holidays are key milestones in the church year.

It can help churches think about their use of time if they conduct an audit of the time needed to run the activities of the church. For each activity a list of those involved is made and the time they give either in a typical week or typical month is noted. Looking across the different activities of the church it is possible to see which individuals are giving most time. With this overview it is also possible for the church to think about how the use of time matches the priorities that the church has identified.

In the Exploration section of this chapter, I described four categories of participation – nuclear, modal, marginal and dormant – and suggested that each church has its own definitions of those categories. Some church councils find it helpful to reflect what proportion of those who attend belong to the different categories. This can also generate a discussion about whether the thresholds between the categories need to be redrawn or better communicated.

A final comment: I have put this chapter first because I consider time to be the most significant resource for the local church. However, I readily admit that it can generate the most tense discussions and so it may not be the right one to discuss first if the book is being used by a small group.

Further reading

Church Urban Fund (2008), *Just Employment*, London: Church Urban Fund.
   Online resource giving guidance on employing paid staff. See www. cufx.org.uk
Bunting, M. (2004), *Willing Slaves: How the Overwork Culture is Ruling Our Lives*, London: HarperCollins.
   A journalist's account of how changing working culture is affecting personal life.
Francis, L. J. and P. Richter (2007), *Gone for Good? Church-Leaving and Returning in the 21st Century*, Peterborough: Epworth Press.
   Readable analysis of reasons for leaving the church, including issues of time.

Fryar, A., R. Jackson, et al. (eds) (2007), *Turn Your Organisation into a Volunteer Magnet*, published by editors.
Numerous suggestions for attracting volunteers. See www.volunteering.org.uk/Resources

Restall, M. (2005), *Volunteers and the Law*, London: Volunteering England.
A guide to the legal issues in working with volunteers. See www.volunteering.org.uk/Resources

Notes

1 See Appendix B at the end of the book for examples of statistics that illustrate these points. They can help congregations gauge how close to the average their experience is.

2 For a further discussion of this, see H. Cameron, P. Richter et al. (eds), *Studying Local Churches: A Handbook*, London, SCM Press, 2005, pp. 160–5.

3 Large numbers of people are able to recite: 'Be near me, Lord Jesus; I ask thee to stay close by me for ever, and love me, I pray; bless all the dear children in thy tender care, and fit us for heaven to live with thee there' (Anon, nineteenth century).

4 One example of this is the number of TV property shows that cut in a picture of a parish church to indicate the desirable nature of a particular property or neighbourhood.

4

Money

Introduction

The purpose of this chapter is to look at the way in which money acts as a resource in church life. Like time, this is a sensitive resource to discuss. Discussion of personal finances beyond immediate family members is unusual in the UK. After a case study, the Exploration section discusses the different sources of income a church can draw upon. Two theological fragments are offered for reflection. The chapter concludes with a discussion of the way in which each cultural form of church makes use of money, and suggestions for further reading.

Experience

Barnabus Methodist Church

The ravages of the Second World War and subsequent town planning have been kind to Barnabus Methodist Church. Like many Methodist churches, its sprawling Victorian buildings were located on a side road off the High Street. However, the realignment of the town centre around the glass and concrete shopping centre made the entrance to the church hall a prime location right opposite the shopping centre.

Ten years ago, after some energetic fundraising, the church hall was reordered with a cafe facing onto the street. From the start there was a desire to do things properly and match the quality of furnishings, food and presentation in commercial coffee shops. This meant having two paid people on duty whenever the cafe was open, one supervising the kitchen, the other the service. The prices are not a lot less than commercial cafes but trade is brisk and it has brought new people through the door.

Five years ago, the local health authority asked the church if it could run a session for young mums in an adjacent room while the cafe was open. Then a mental health charity asked if they could run a support meeting. There were extensive discussions in the committee that oversaw the cafe as to whether the prices should be reduced to accommodate these new visitors. A compromise emerged of a menu within a menu. A cup of tea or coffee is much cheaper than a pot of tea or coffee for one. Buttered toast was introduced at a low price, but toasted teacakes retained at their original price. This strategy worked well and the wider range of people using the cafe blended in and enjoyed the friendliness of the volunteers.

Three years ago, the District Development Enabler suggested that the cafe would make a good venue for an Alpha course. Three courses were held, attracting mainly the 'tea and toast' customers of the cafe. This then evolved into a cafe church meeting on Wednesday evenings with informal discussions, prayer and a meal.

At a recent church council meeting, one of the lay leaders expressed disappointment that the new Christians at the Cafe Church had not joined the church properly. This sparked a debate with some arguing that the Cafe Church could be 'proper church' for those who had no previous experience of church. Then someone suggested that if the Cafe Church was becoming a real church, its members should be paying more than the cost of their meal.

Exploration

In many local churches an understanding of finance is left in a few hands. This can be because it is seen as an area needing expertise and so the preserve of those with the appropriate knowledge, or because it is seen as the aspect of church life furthest removed from the spiritual or 'real' purposes of the church.

I want to argue that the way in which a church gains its income and what it spends it on can tell you about its understanding of mission. The French sociologist Pierre Bourdieu (1998) has noted that the finances of the church are more like those of a household than of a business. There is an economy of gifts as well as contact with the market economy, and there is usually a mix of paid and unpaid work. There can be ambivalent feelings about the relationship of the paid work to the market economy and a need to present it as 'more than that'. This can mean that those who do paid work for the church receive a less than fair livelihood.

The suspicion of money is understandable. Some would want to argue that money has taken on a god-like role in society (Goodchild, 2007), and that we are consumed by the things we purchase. The market can be seen as diminishing our sense of agency by creating a direct link between desire for something and its purchase without the intervening step of decision-making about whether the desired good is beneficial to our flourishing or the flourishing of the environment. Those dealing with money on behalf of the church can be seen as 'getting entangled in everyday affairs'.[1]

Another factor affecting the way in which money is perceived is the gradual decline in what sociologists call 'generalized social trust' (Anheier and Kendall, 2002; Grenier and Wright, 2006): that is, our willingness to give money to institutions to spend on our behalf. Now people tend to be more willing to give if they know the money will go directly to a person or cause they have chosen. This has affected church members' willingness to give through denominational structures or agencies. Within the local church a decline in social trust may erode serial reciprocity and replace it with direct reciprocity. Serial reciprocity is the doing of a good turn knowing that it is likely to be returned at some unknown point in the future.

An example would be giving an elderly church member a lift to the services knowing that when you reach that age there will be someone who will do the same for you. Direct reciprocity means doing a good turn knowing when it will be returned and in what kind. An example would be taking someone's child to a church event knowing that the next week they will be taking your child to a swimming lesson.

I would want to argue for avoiding the temptations associated with money by understanding it and discussing it. Stuart Murray (2000), in his fascinating critique of tithing, suggests that having a rule about giving avoids the more difficult discussions about our own use of money and the priorities that reveals in our own lives. He argues for churches where there are relationships of sufficient trust and accountability to have private conversations about how members are using their money and from that will flow the necessary discussions about the financial priorities of the church.

The rest of this section looks at the different sources of income that churches draw upon as a way of provoking discussion about their relative importance in the life of your church.

Member giving

Most local churches have a culture of giving that shapes the extent of member giving and the way in which it is organized. Some churches do set an expectation, such as a tithe, as a guide to their members as to how much to give. Others will distinguish between giving to support the day-to-day running of the church and giving for particular causes or projects. Giving to religious causes is one of the largest areas of committed personal giving.[2] However, the distribution of giving in a church is often uneven, with a small proportion of donors giving a substantial proportion of the money.[3]

Gift aid

Most local churches have systems for reclaiming gift aid on money given by members who are taxpayers. The administration for this may be done locally or centrally but it does require methodical record-keeping. Murray (2000) argues that it is inappropriate to reclaim tax on money that is used to fund facilities from which one personally benefits. However, the retention of religion as a charitable object suggests that the state is willing to contribute to the costs of religious institutions.[4]

Levies or donations from small groups

Some churches encourage a contribution from small groups that use their premises, which goes towards the costs of maintenance and utilities. This can mean that church members pay in a number of different ways towards the costs, but it can also spread the costs to non-members who belong to these groups.

Intra-denominational funding

Most local churches that belong to a denomination participate in some form of cross-subsidising whereby richer churches help poorer churches. In some denominations the system is centrally prescribed, in others there are extensive negotiations about the level of payment and the criteria by which the payment is assessed. Decline in generalized social trust has affected compliance with these systems. More pointed questions are asked about why poor churches are poor, and the indicators used to measure the resources of the church are sometimes modified. Churches who are reluctant compliers with intra-denominational funding may be generous in other ways, such as funding one of their members to do development work overseas. Churches who are recipients of intra-denominational funding may feel as if they are falling short of expectations. This can be particularly acute when there are theological differences between cash-rich and cash-poor churches or where a magnet church is attracting people of working age from other local churches.

External funding

Some churches are adept at seeking external funding for their community activities or to maintain their buildings. This is often because they have a minister or member who knows about fundraising or because they are willing to seek advice from the denominational officers or infrastructure organizations there for that purpose. External funding can be time-consuming to obtain, and the energy invested is often met with disappointment. Once received, money often carries particular accountability requirements that have to be accommodated alongside the church's existing ways of managing money. External funders put a premium on the innovative and so there can be a weariness in seeking to describe work that meets a demonstrable need as somehow breaking new ground.

Trading and letting

Some churches generate income through trading activities, such as cafes or letting their premises to non-church groups. Such activities require prices to be set or negotiated and so the church has to become aware of the value of what it supplies in the local economy. It is then faced with decisions about whether to charge less or the same as the market value. Church buildings usually have reduced local taxes and so commercial traders can be resentful of competition that is in effect working with reduced overheads. Calculating a price usually raises questions of cost. Costs can be calculated in a minimalist way including only the additional cost of utilities or they can be calculated in a more comprehensive way to include a share of maintaining the building and depreciation of equipment used. The ability of churches to provide premises at a modest cost is often an overlooked service they provide to the community. It provides an incubator in which new and fragile activities can get off the ground and test their viability. Some churches vary the price they charge according to the support they wish to give to the group concerned.

Member-to-member fundraising

My sense is that this is a declining area of income in many churches. Fetes, coffee mornings, jumble sales, concerts, sales of work all rely for their fundraising success on the voluntary donation of goods and the volunteering of time to make them happen. The chapter on time has signalled that much of the time that these activities relied upon has evaporated. Many churches would have had an auction of harvest produce (home-grown vegetables and home-made food) following a harvest supper. It is more likely now that people will give tins bought as part of their weekly shopping, which will be donated to a local homelessness charity. There may be new ways round this difficulty, for example members taking part in sponsored activities and inviting online sponsorship, some of which will go to a church-related cause. But again, the request for money is likely to be more specific and not money that the church can use to fund its general running costs.

Interest

For some churches the bank interest on their 'rainy day' fund or on a past legacy helps balance the books. This is clearly dependent upon fluctuations in interest rates. Over-reliance on this source of income can lead to the capital sum never being used for its intended purposes.

Fundraising from the public

Many member-to-member fundraising activities were designed to attract the public and some, such as concerts and fetes, will do that still. Some churches do have 'Friends of' organizations that raise money on their behalf or they have contact details for people who use their building for community activities and seek to involve them in fundraising. Churches can underestimate the way in which local people value the heritage or community amenity of their building and do not seek to engage in this type of fundraising.

Legacies and in memoriam fundraising

Legacies are invested in catch-up repairs to buildings or the purchase of an item (such as an organ) that would require extensive fundraising otherwise. People often give generously at funerals and again churches can give specific opportunities for families to contribute to the church.

Church members often have a low awareness of how their money is being spent.

The main categories include:

- ministerial salaries and housing
- other salaries
- costs of maintaining buildings and equipment
- utilities
- contributing to denominational costs
- charitable giving, both within and beyond the denomination.

Finally, churches sometimes have a low awareness of their assets and their current market value. Sometimes insurance values are used as a proxy and this can obscure the true value of an under-used asset. Many denominations have a system for appraising the state of buildings every five years to ensure they are being kept in good repair. It is less common to do this with equipment and other assets.

Resources for reflection

This section offers two theological fragments to stimulate reflection. The first brings together a parable and story from Matthew's discussions of accountability and judgement. The second reflects upon the doctrine of sin.

Bible

The faithful stewards (Matthew 25.14–30)

The costly perfume (Matthew 26.6–13)

Stewardship has become associated with financial caution, with not spending more than is absolutely necessary and keeping plenty by for a rainy day. The parable depicts stewards who run the household in the master's absence and are expected to make a return on funds entrusted to them and not just put them in a bank or under a mattress. This cannot be achieved without risk. It would have been good to know what the master would have said to a steward who had taken a risk that did not pay off and had nothing to hand back. Trustworthiness includes deploying the master's assets.

Where does the caution in managing church finances come from? Is it worry about irresponsible ordained ministers with over-ambitious ideas that they won't be around to reap? Is it a fear of decline in giving as members get older? Is it fear of a rainy day when something unforeseen goes wrong and we are not prepared? Hauerwas (2007, p. 210) suggests that the parable is a judgement 'against those who think they deserve what they have earned, as well as those who do not know how precious is the gift they have been given'.

In the story of the unknown woman with the costly perfume, we don't know what proportion of her total resources the jar of ointment represented. She may have sold her own possessions to buy this gift. Or did this jar represent her rainy day fund – something she could cash in to meet unexpected adversity? Jesus commends her for recognizing that this is a moment that will pass – his physical presence will not always be with them. The physical form of the church is changing. Some churches are facing the recognition that the form they have known and loved will pass away in their lifetime. It can be painful to recognize that that moment has come. Is there a moment at which extravagance is justified and preparation can be made for the death of what is, knowing that the possibility of a new form of life remains? Joe Kapolyo, in the *Africa Bible Commentary* (Adeyemo, 2006, p. 1165), likens this unknown woman to Lydia (Acts 16.14–15) who puts the resources of her household at the disposal of the gospel. Lydia has to balance the requirements of her business, her household and the emerging church. The balancing and discernment required of those who steward the resources of the church today seems no less demanding.

Doctrine

Sin

Money is a powerful source of temptation because it presents us with choices. Robert R. Williams (Hodgson and King, 2008, ch. 7) offers three understandings of sin, each of which suggests different ways in which a church might be tempted to mis-value money.

The first understanding of sin is that it is a refusal to accept that we are finite creatures dependent upon an infinite creator. We are tempted to seek independence and may believe that money can buy us that independence. If we have sufficient resources then we can avoid dependence upon other parts of the church. This in turn loosens our obligations to other parts of the church. If we don't need them, why should we help pay for them?

The second understanding is that as humans we can put ourselves in the place of the transcendent and so try to secure our own survival. This can lead to pride and self-seeking with projects that boost the egos of leaders. More often it leads to extreme caution as we avoid any risk that would get in the way of a safe journey to the end of another financial year.

The third understanding of sin is that, having replaced a trust in the transcendent with a trust in our own ability to secure the future, we spend money in a way that bolsters the identity we have chosen. Money is used to differentiate us from other churches rather than starting with our missional essence.

Sin in the church is rarely a seeking of evil for its own sake. More often it is a corrupted seeking of a genuine good – a deflection from the mission of God.

Planning for practice

This section looks at the logic of the five cultural forms of church when applied to their relationship with money. It concludes with some suggested ways of discussing church finances.

Parish

The logic of a public utility is that everyone contributes according to their income or property value. Indeed a system of tithing was in force on behalf of the established church until the nineteenth century. Something that is available to everyone in their immediate neighbourhood is paid for by everyone. The logic of a private utility is that those who use the service pay a fee for its use. Parish churches usually do charge for the occasional offices but the fees charged severely underestimate the cost of maintaining the building and paying clergy so that they are available when needed. As with all utilities, the temptation is to leave the costs of the infrastructure not fully calculated. Repairs accumulate and depreciation money is not set aside to upgrade fixtures and fittings. The logic of the parish is that the wider population should contribute. The last chapter mentioned 'Friends of' groups. It may be possible to be more rigorous in inviting donations alongside fees. I would want to lobby for a heritage tax to be paid as an element of council tax. It could be argued that the National Lottery has taken us some way in that direction although it is more regressive than a property-based tax. Most parishes rely in large part on the voluntary giving of their regular attenders but this could be seen as an accident of history unless they are now understood to be the main beneficiaries of its services. This is not to negate the values of stewardship given theological emphasis in denominations with parish polities.

Gathered congregation

At one level, the funding of a voluntary association by subscriptions and the funding of a gathered congregation by giving feel like very different models. In practice, most local voluntary associations derive a significant part of their income from other sources, such as a surplus made on running events, a surplus on goods supplied in connection with their activity, member-to-member fundraising and interest on deposits. Members often make donations beyond their subscriptions to help younger people in the association or to memorialize members who have died. These other sources of income would be familiar to gathered churches. Voluntary associations are also likely to have a culture of paying subscriptions. This includes a period of unpaid subs before membership is revoked, a policy of not reminding members who are known to be in financial difficulties and of dropping hints to family members that next year's sub might make a good present. This is not unlike the culture of giving that exists in gathered churches. Where it breaks down is where there are persistent non-contributors who enjoy the benefits of membership but don't contribute anything other than token amounts of money. Many denominations employ stewardship advisers whose job it is to go into local churches and try to shift the culture of giving.

Small-group church

One of the attractions of small groups is their ability to get by without much money changing hands. A lot of weekly requirements can be met by giving in kind. The meeting will take place at one person's house, with another supplying the refreshments, a third person keeping the children occupied and another person offering lifts. These gifts in kind can be rotated between members so no one bears an unfair burden. The close relationships that develop in small groups often extend to acts of informal care. This replicates the gift economy of the household. Norms of generosity and reciprocity are established by example and negotiation.

There can be different ways of funding the church beyond the small group. In top-down models there is considerable loyalty to the centre, which is often aligned with the ministry of a particular leader. Money is readily given to support this ministry and the teaching that flows from it. In bottom-up models the centre is seen more as an agency, there to do those things that the small groups can't do for themselves.

Third-place church

Third-place church can often survive by charging an entrance or sessional fee or by selling refreshments at commercial prices. This covers the costs of the venue, any hospitality and the incidental expenses of the leaders. The funding of this model becomes more complex when the church has its own premises or paid leadership. Price is one of the key signals that a third place uses to establish its identity. Charging the wrong price or, worse, not charging at all suggests that the value of the event or experience is not properly understood. Once a third-place church starts to provide something more than an event at a venue, the simplicity of its economic model can waver and more associational claims are made on its participants.

Magnet church

Magnet churches tend to attract families who are cash rich and time poor. As the last chapter said, the equation between time and money is well understood and a third variable of quality is also factored in. Giving as part of participation in church is often only one element of buying into a subculture of parenting that allows children and teenagers to have normal lives but within an ethically bounded world. Examples of parallel activities include Christian music festivals, activity holidays and performing arts groups with their associated music, websites and t-shirts. Rather like making use of private education, it is well understood that more than the monthly direct debit is required. There are extras, such as affinity clothing and member-to-member fundraising. There will be less embarrassment in a magnet church in spelling out the culture of giving and its expectations.

Where it is not done on an annual basis, it can be a helpful aid to decision-making for a church to look at an analysis of its income, expenditure and assets.[5] Agreeing the categories under which this should be done is in itself a useful indication of priorities. This sort of analysis can also be a basis for asking four questions commonly used by voluntary organizations:

- Are resources being used in an economical way, avoiding waste?
- Are resources being used in an efficient way, gaining the best value for money spent?
- Are resources being used in an effective way, enabling the church to achieve its purposes?
- Are resources being used in an equitable way, recognising the claims of the local and wider church, community and environment?

But there are some even tougher questions that churches can ask themselves:

- If the five people who give most leave, by what percentage will our income from giving decrease?
- What is the cost of running our building for each hour it is open?
- What are the trends in our income and expenditure for the last five years?

These are not easy questions to ask and it can be helpful to separate the discussion into three phases: first, how to analyse the data; second, how to interpret the analysis; and, third, a discussion about its interpretation and significance.

Further reading

Durran, M. (2003), *The UK Church Fundraising Handbook: A Practical Manual and Directory of Sources*, Norwich: Canterbury Press.
A comprehensive guide to fundraising for churches.
Grieve, J. (1999), *Fundraising for Churches*, London: SPCK.
A guide to fundraising for church projects.
Poffley, A. (2002), *Financial Stewardship of Charities: Maximising Impact in Times of Uncertainty*, London: Directory of Social Change.
A clear statement of principles and processes for running charity finances.
The following website has resources on stewardship: www.parishresources.org.uk.

Notes

1 2 Timothy 2.4: 'No one serving in the army gets entangled in everyday affairs; the soldier's aim is to please the enlisting officer' (NRSV).

2 See S. Clegg, L. Goodey et al., *UK Giving 2008*, London, CAF and NCVO, 2008. An annual report available at www.cafonline.org. While 20 per cent of donors give to medical research compared to 7 per cent of donors giving to religious causes, 18 per cent of all charitable giving goes to religious causes compared to 15 per cent of giving to medical research. Donors to religious causes give an average mean donation of £44 a month.

3 The report *Giving for Life*, put before the July 2009 Church of England Synod (GS 1723), stated that 10 per cent of givers were giving in a planned way a proportion of their income. Their contributions amounted to one-third of donated income.

4 See the following report for guidance: Charity Commission, *The Advancement of Religion for the Public Benefit*, Charity Commission, 2008. It can be downloaded from www.charitycommission.gov. uk/publicbenefit.

5 For further discussion of this, see H. Cameron, P. Richter et al. (eds), *Studying Local Churches: A Handbook*, London, SCM Press, 2005, pp. 165–7.

5

Buildings

Introduction

The purpose of this chapter is to look at the part that buildings play in resourcing mission. After an opening case study the context is explored. Two theological fragments are offered and then the different use of buildings by the five different cultural forms of church is discussed. Further reading is suggested.

Experience

Christchurch

Christchurch was started 35 years ago as an offshoot of the local Baptist church. There had been some disagreements about charismatic renewal, and those drawn to its spirituality left and formed Christchurch. Meeting initially in homes, after a few years a redundant Independent Chapel, not far from the market place, had been purchased. Fifteen years ago the church started to grow quite rapidly. This coincided with the building of a new motorway that brought two conurbations within commuting distance of the market town in which Christchurch is located. Much of the growth came from families moving into the town seeking a better quality of life, including a good school and a good church. The founding leadership team of Christchurch had included two schoolteachers, and so there had always been a strong emphasis on programmes for children and teenagers. These programmes became more extensive as the church grew.

Everyone agreed that the chapel was now too small for their activities and that with the shops so busy on a Sunday, parking was a nightmare. The leadership team spent a lot of time looking at how the chapel and its site could be redeveloped to make a space and facilities more appropriate for work with children. The cost of the plan was just over £1m. The treasurer agreed that it sounded a lot of money, but pointed out that if every family attending the church was to put an extra £20,000 on their mortgage they would have the money tomorrow.

Jenny, a member of the leadership team, wondered if there was another way. She was governor of the prep school both her sons attended. In an off-the-record discussion with the bursar she realized the school was keen to diversify its sources of income as an insurance against the roll falling. They would be open to renting the school to Christchurch at evenings and weekends. Jenny felt this would give them the child-friendly premises they sought and solve the parking problem at a stroke. She also hoped that more families from the school would be attracted to the church. If they sold their present building, they could employ a full-time administrator to free up the pastor's time and employ a second youth worker for the older teens.

At the next leadership team meeting she shared her solution. John, one of the founding members of the church, was horrified. Why waste money on rent when you could own your own premises? How would people know about the church if it was no longer in the town centre? But Jenny's idea sparked the imagination of others and by the end of the evening the leadership team was divided.

Exploration

Expectations of public buildings have changed considerably in the last twenty years. Warmth, comfort, cleanliness, provision of refreshments, toilets, parking and special facilities for those with young children or people with a disability are now standard. Many of our public spaces, such as shopping centres, leisure centres, cinemas and stations are now run by the private sector who wish to make them more enticing spaces in which to spend money and so have increased their comfort. Sites that convey the history of the country are now often presented as heritage visitor attractions with a range of interpretative media accompanied by cafe, gift shop, toilets and parking.[1]

The diversity of church buildings is immense and so this section covers some of the roles they perform, recognizing that not every church building will perform every role. Some churches have followed the market in seeing their buildings as public space and/or heritage site and in seeking to match expectations that have been created elsewhere. Others either consciously or unconsciously resist this.

Winston Churchill said, 'We shape our buildings, and afterwards our buildings shape us.'[2] Church buildings are things we seek to shape to reflect our faith and things which we allow to shape us through the possibilities for worship, fellowship and service they offer or constrain. Decisions about buildings can be the most costly and momentous a church takes and so having conversations about how the role of the building in the life of the church is understood can be vital in securing a basis for change.

Churches can be oases of quietness and greenery. A survey done for the Church of England (Church Heritage Forum, 2004) reports that 19 per cent of people seek out a church building for quiet, and this rises to 40 per cent in city centres. Churchyards and the gardens in church grounds can be lungs of green in urban environments, with trees, flowers, butterflies and birds.[3] These aspects of churches link to a wider holistic spirituality that wishes to connect with self and with nature. Alongside these positive features, churches can have concerns about vandalism and security. There can be a tension between a desire to be open to the casual visitor and maintain security.

Many but not all church buildings have something to tell of the history of their locality and some have a wider historical significance. Most of these will be listed in order to secure the features of historical interest. This can be a lever for fundraising to support the fabric of the church, but it can also restrict what a church would like to do with its building for its current purposes. Negotiating an appropriate balance between those whose primary interest is historical and those whose primary interest is contemporary can be difficult. One focus for shared energy is the quality of the materials available to interpret the building to its visitors. A number of emphases are possible: the historical and aesthetic significance of the building, its role in local and national history, how its Christian symbolism relates to its current use. Interpretative materials increasingly need to contain explanations of terms which, while familiar to church-goers, may not be understood by the wider population.

Information that links the church to other buildings that can be visited and to local facilities, including refreshments, parking and toilets, can help meet expectations that the church itself may not be able to satisfy. Making this information available on the Internet and in tourist information offices for those looking for places of interest can increase visitor numbers.

Churches buildings can also be sites of formal and informal education. Interpretative materials aimed at children and related appropriately to the national curriculum can be a stimulus for school visits. Even buildings of little historical interest can be used to tell the Christian story.[4] These materials can also be made available when the church is open to visitors, enabling all generations in a visiting family to engage with the building.

Church buildings can be both venues and bases for cultural activities. As venues for concerts, plays and exhibitions they can offer an affordable space that is already well known locally. They can provide rehearsal space for groups that support the worship of the church, such as choirs and bands, but they can also host other groups. Churches continue to commission artefacts and decorative items for their buildings and these can exemplify local craftsmanship and continue to weave the story of the community into the story of the building. These commissions can be important ways of enculturating the gospel in aesthetic forms that speak to those not steeped in the Christian story.

Some sociologists and historians who study secularization (Brown, 2001; Taylor, 2007) argue that as well as the church having a reduced role in society and religious practice declining, the Christian story has a reduced role in shaping culture and everyday categories of thought. If this is so, then the heritage, educational and cultural aspects of church buildings are crucial points of access for those wishing to understand the Christian story and its past and present significance.

Church buildings often remain in communities when other facilities are sparse. In rural communities they sometimes offer space for the shop or post office (Grieve, Jochum et al., 2007; Gaze, 2006). In urban communities, they can be a base for service provision and so contribute to the regeneration of the community (Farnell, Furbey et al., 2003; Torry, 2007). Church buildings can be important locations for the encounters that build social capital in a community, that is, those relationships that can be called upon in time of need (Baker, 2009).

Church buildings remain places where families can celebrate and commemorate their lives in public whether through baptisms/dedications, weddings, funerals, memorial services, Christmas, Harvest or Mothers' Day. The association of those celebrations with particular buildings is part of the store of memory (Hervieu-Leger, 2000). It also links families to others who have shared the same occasions in the same building.

Part of what a church building can offer to a community is a set of premises that can host other activities that the community values (Finneron and Dinham, 2002). This can include hosting other congregations that don't have their own premises, hosting voluntary or community organizations, either with office space or for their activities, providing space for workers in a range of welfare services to meet clients, and a space for public meetings.

The role of church buildings in supporting activities of benefit to the local community is increasingly recognized by policy-makers. However, there can be tensions with policy agendas that seek to place local people in greater ownership and control of local facilities (Aiken, Cairns et al., 2008). The responsibility for church buildings is usually in the control of the governance structures of the church. These may involve substantial numbers of local people, who will not have been chosen because of where they live but because of their part in the life of the church. Some but not all churches will have democratic mechanisms for including the wider voice of church members in those decisions. Few churches have mechanisms for consulting the whole community on their policies towards their building.

Having set out this wide and demanding set of purposes which can shape the use of church buildings, it is hardly surprising that the work of maintaining and repairing church buildings figures so largely in the life of many churches. It can feel as if all the time and money of the church is focused on the building. The material provided in this section is with the aim of constantly raising the question 'To what purpose?' Our familiarity with the church buildings we use can make us blind to both their potential and their faults. It can be hard to hear the views of an outsider or newcomer about a much-loved building, but their perceptions are valuable if we hope that the building will be used by people beyond current worshippers.

Finally, it is important to remember those churches that do not own their own building either by choice or through lack of resources. They still have a relationship with the building they use and have to negotiate their needs alongside its primary purpose. The financial costs of owning a building can be replaced by the additional time needed to prepare the building for church uses. The relationship with the primary user can become frayed if there is not regular face-to-face contact because the church uses the building at times when its regular users are absent. However, not having a building also provides the opportunity to enculturate the gospel into a mundane setting, leaving traces of the Christian story in a secular context.

Resources for reflection

Bible

Martha and Mary (Luke 10.38–42)

Tom Wright (2001, pp. 125–32) argues that this story is about the use of space in the household. A small home would have had an outer room in which the men of the family entertained guests and an inner room where women would have prepared food and cared for children. Only in the bedroom would husband and wife sleep together with their children around them. In order to learn from the rabbi, as any male disciple would, Mary enters the public space and leaves behind her domestic duties. Jesus asserts that the public role of disciple will not be taken away from Mary. He urges Martha not to be consumed by her domestic responsibilities.

Catherine Booth, one of the founders of the Salvation Army, is reputed to have said that she felt more at home in the pulpit than in the kitchen. She also complained that it was impossible to write sermons and keep up with all the sewing she needed to do for her large family (Green, 1997). Jennifer Smith (2006) has pointed out that the pulpit and the kitchen can represent different sources of authority in a church building, with people gravitating towards one or the other. But gender is only one way of demarcating space. Many church buildings have distinctions between sacred and mundane space, sometimes even with separate entrances from the street. Our understanding of church buildings comes in part from the way in which those buildings are used. The boundaries they contain and the messages those boundaries are designed to convey may be intentional but they can also act as points of unintentional exclusion.

Harvey (2004, p. 246) points out that the phrase, 'there is need of only one thing' has mystified commentators. What is the one thing that is needed in this situation? Buildings generate their own distractions and worries. It is easy to lose sight of their purpose or to stop asking, 'What is the one purpose they serve at this particular moment of the week?' At the moment of hospitality, can we set aside the distractions of keeping a building prepared, to focus on the guests who enter?

Doctrine

Sacrament and sacramentality

Stephen W. Sykes (Hodgson and King, 2008, ch. 10) suggests that the understanding of sacrament in the Christian tradition can be placed on a spectrum from objective to subjective. Those with an objective understanding see the sacraments as a work of God's grace irrespective of the response of the believer. Those with a subjective understanding see them as an opportunity to receive grace by responding with faith.

The understanding of church buildings can be seen as falling along a similar spectrum. Some would understand an objective need for a sacred space in which to worship. Others would argue that any space can be experienced as revealing God's presence. The objectivists would argue for the sense of God being more accessible in places that have been used for prayer for a long time. Subjectivists would want to focus on the possibility of recognizing God in any circumstance.

How important is the sign in evoking the sacramental encounter? For some it will be essential, for others incidental. Some will want to worship in a building that is a sign to them of God's presence. That sign might arise from the building's long use, its aesthetic qualities, or its personal associations with their life, or a combination of these factors. Others will deliberately seek to worship in buildings that have other uses, such as pubs, schools or village halls, as a way of bringing God's presence into the world. Any symbolism will be concentrated in objects rather than the building itself.

Sykes notes that signs carry within them readings other than those intended by the liturgist. The Eucharist can be read as a sign of justice or of hierarchy. The same might be said of church buildings. The noticeboard may say 'All welcome' but if the adaptations for disabled people are tokenistic, another reading might be made.

Sacraments are social and indicate participation in the body of Christ as a social reality. The layout and use of church buildings can hinder or help the relational fellowship of the church. Can all generations mix freely? Are there spaces for quiet conversation as well as socializing? What social understanding of the church does the worship space convey?

Planning for practice

The five cultural forms each have their own logic when it comes to the ownership and use of buildings. However, church life evolves and so there are many churches that are seeking to enact a particular form in a building that comes from another model. So, as in the case of Barnabus Methodist Church in the previous chapter, a third-place church has developed in the premises of a gathered congregation. This section concludes with some suggestions for starting the conversation about buildings.

Parish

A parish church, whether Anglican, Church of Scotland or Roman Catholic, is seen as part of the landscape by the population that relates to it. Like a public utility, the church building is part of the infrastructure of the community. A landscape without roads, drains, telegraph poles and pylons would look empty in a way we couldn't initially put our finger on, because they are taken for granted. The architecture of church buildings clearly marks them out as sacred space. Their purpose is as self-evident as that of a road. As the last chapter pointed out, failing to maintain infrastructure is a frequent strategy for utilities when funds are short. An aspect of parish churches in particular is that they were designed in another time, for the religious needs of the community as understood then.[5] Also their number and size can bear little relationship to the population as it is dispersed now. All this can place a substantial responsibility on the shoulders of a few. The last chapter suggested 'Friends of' groups as a way of broadening that sense of responsibility for this part of the community infrastructure. There may be people who want to distance themselves from religious observance but who none the less have chosen to live in a community because of its character and readily admit that the church contributes to that. Sharing information about the reality of maintaining the fabric of the building with the wider community could be seen as part of the church's stewardship of the building. The fact that parish churches are often open for people to use as quiet space also adds to this wider sense of ownership. The physical focal points in parish churches are usually altar, pulpit and font, speaking of their sacramental and liturgical purposes.

Gathered congregations

Gathered congregations meet in a huge variety of buildings, some of historic interest and listed, others in fairly unattractive buildings erected at the same time as the housing that surrounds them, and some in reordered or new buildings that seek to meet a range of needs for both church and community. Despite this variety, these buildings have the feel of being owned and managed by the church but thrown open, in a hospitable way, to the surrounding community. They blur public and private space by taking responsibility for a threshold over which people can be invited. It is unusual for the buildings of gathered churches to be open as quiet spaces. They are more usually open for activities, but otherwise locked. Many gathered congregations are in buildings that served the needs of earlier generations and are a struggle for the present numbers using them to maintain. Gathered congregations can be creative in reordering their buildings to combine a number of functions alongside maintaining sacred space. The focal points in these buildings are usually the pulpit in the sacred space and the kitchen in the mundane space.

Small-group church

Small-group church has two meeting places, the homes where small groups meet and the larger buildings used for whole-church worship and events. The building used for whole-church gatherings may be owned or rented on a sessional basis. Where the building is owned it is likely to be hired out as meeting space. Owning a building can create pressures to move to a gathered-church model where the building is the hub of activity. The use of homes is an advantage in not generating overheads for the church. It can create pressures for members in terms of the presentation of their home and the supplying of refreshments. The home is a significant site for our consumption of goods that indicate our social and economic status, not least the location of the home. Where small groups have members from different neighbourhoods and different socio-economic backgrounds there tend to be norms of hospitality that are modest and attainable by all group members. Such groups may also choose to meet in a third place to bypass the visible symbols of difference that their homes convey. The focal point of meetings in the home tend to be the lounge or living room in which meetings take place and the kitchen as a space for more private conversations.

Third-place church

Third-place churches meet in public spaces that they usually do not own or manage. Third spaces offer the advantage of a space that no one owns and so provide a stage for more egalitarian encounters. However, third spaces are designed to signal a market niche and so have features that exclude as well as include. Location is crucial to the identity of a third place. It needs to respond to the buildings around it and reflect the needs of the users of those buildings. The national coffee chains signal their understanding of a location as 'on the way up' by locating in places that attract 'their kind of customer'. The furnishing and ambiance of the interior also send out signals as to who the place is for. Churches can deliberately set out to subvert the market by creating third places for people who would be marginalized from commercial third places, such as parents with very young children or the homeless. Third places are interesting in that the focal point is usually the counter at which refreshments are served, but this is incidental to the way in which the space is used. Usually the furniture can be moved to accommodate conversations of various sizes and levels of intimacy and so the focal point is the conversation, which can happen in different places at different visits. There is an attachment to the location but also a detachment from the practical realities of the place. Participants can relax as guests without feeling that at some point they may be expected to become the host.

Magnet church

Magnet churches tend to meet either in buildings they have inherited from parish or gathered-church models or in functional buildings which are suitable for their style of worship. Inherited buildings are often reordered so that the worshippers face the longest wall. Functional buildings may be hired rather than owned. Parking is often a key issue and so functional buildings may have an out-of-town location. Any aesthetic adornment of the building is usually temporary and changed on a regular basis. The focal point of the building is the screen used for multi-media presentations in worship and other meetings. Warmth, comfort, appropriate toilet and catering facilities are important. Sacredness comes from the nature of the gathering rather than the texture of the building.

The prospect of changing a building to enable it to serve a local church's understanding of mission is daunting. There are many plates to be kept spinning at the same time: the views of those who belong to the local church; the views of the local community; the requirements of the denomination; the requirements of local planning authorities; plus the requirements of funders.

Existing users of a building are often comfortable with it and can struggle to see the need for change. It is hoped that discussions of this book might help pave the way for change. However, there are simple activities that can promote thought:

- getting church members to stand outside the building at different points in the week and observe how many and what sort of people walk past;
- visiting the buildings of other churches who have tried out ideas similar to the ones you are contemplating;
- calculating the cost of running the building for each hour it is in use;
- asking people visiting the building for the first time for their impressions of it.

By observing what is happening, it becomes possible to ask why it is happening and how it serves the church's understanding of mission.

Seeking external advice can also be a valuable trigger for change and the resources listed below, plus those from denominations, can be of help.

Further reading

Bond, P. (2006), *Open for You: The Church, the Visitor and the Gospel*, Norwich: Canterbury Press.
A guide to opening churches and making the public welcome.
Church Heritage Forum (2004), *Building Faith in our Future*, London: Church House Publishing.
www.cofe.anglican.org/about/builtheritage/buildingfaith/report.
pdf
Discussion of policy relating to church buildings.
Durran, M. (2005), *Making Church Buildings Work: A Handbook for Managing and Developing Church Buildings for Mission and Ministry*, Norwich: Canterbury Press.
A treasure trove of practical guidance.
Durran, M. (2006), *Regenerating Local Churches: Mission-Based Strategies for Transformation and Growth*, Norwich: Canterbury Press.

Guidance on projects designed to facilitate community use of church buildings.

Giles, R. (2004), *Re-pitching the Tent: The Definitive Guide to Reordering Your Church*, Norwich: Canterbury Press.
Advice on reordering church buildings to fit their contemporary liturgical purposes.

Websites

www.churchart.co.uk
Churchart exists to encourage artists, congregations and those involved in the care of churches to foster and engage the arts in the life of the church.

www.churchcare.co.uk
Churchcare is intended to help the people involved in caring for church buildings, through offering practical advice, guidance and links to other useful sources of advice.

www.quietgarden.co.uk
The Quiet Garden Movement encourages the provision of a variety of local venues where there is an opportunity to set aside time to rest and to pray.

www.ecocongregation.org
Eco-congregation is an ecumenical programme helping churches to make the link between environmental issues and Christian faith, and to respond with practical action.

www.onechurch100uses.org/cms
One church, one hundred uses – the website of a community interest company that helps reorder URC churches.

Notes

1 My visit to Rievaulx Abbey, described in Chapter 1, offered all these amenities.

2 'On the night of May 10, 1941, with one of the last bombs of the last serious raid, our House of Commons was destroyed by the violence of the enemy, and we have now to consider whether we should build it up again, and how, and when.

'We shape our buildings, and afterwards our buildings shape us. Having dwelt and served for more than forty years in the late Chamber, and having derived very great pleasure and advantage there from, I, naturally, should like to see it restored in all essentials to its old form, convenience and dignity.'

Source: www.winstonchurchill.org/learn/speeches/quotations

3 See the Quiet Garden Movement for ideas: www.quietgarden. co.uk

4 The Salvation Army has a pack to help its churches arrange school visits. See www.salvationarmy.org.uk and search for 'ultimate school visit'.

5 The Church of England has some 16,000 church buildings with between 12,000 and 13,000 of them listed, that is, recognized by the Government as being of exceptional historic or architectural importance, and about 45 per cent of all Grade I buildings in England are churches. www.cofe.anglican.org/about/builtheritage

6

Risk and Regulation

Introduction

The purpose of this chapter is to look at how the issues of risk and regulation affect the running of the local church. It starts with a case study before exploring the topic. Two theological fragments are offered before the implications of this topic for the five cultural forms of church are explored. Some further reading is suggested.

Experience

Divine Church of God

Winsome and Victor have been members of the Divine Church of God ever since they married 35 years ago. They met in the NHS with Winsome working as a nurse and Victor as a porter. They both retired at 60, glad to escape the physical demands of their jobs and with a sense that the NHS isn't what it was. However, they soon became restless, and the senior pastor, Thomas, encouraged them to play a bigger role in the practical side of church life.

The Divine Church of God owns a former Victorian Methodist church, which they worked hard to buy in the early 1970s. Since then, the building has been maintained by the efforts of its members. The only major reordering was in the mid-1980s when they put in a floor at the level of the first-floor gallery. This created an upstairs worship space but meant that the ground floor could be used for ancillary activities such as Bible classes and their popular supplementary school. The stairs to the gallery are steep and a lift was installed so everyone could reach the worship hall. Twenty years on and the lift is essential as many of the older members are unable to climb the stairs to attend worship.

Winsome and Victor realize they have got involved at just the right time. The church's philosophy of make do and mend was coming into tension with a more modern concern for regulation. The teachers in the supplementary school have had to develop detailed procedures for safeguarding the children, and they have agitated for a more systematic approach to other regulations. Having worked in the NHS Winsome and Victor are aware that there are some rules that apply to everyone. Winsome took the lead in the kitchen, and persuaded everyone who needed to, to do a health and hygiene certificate. Victor galvanized some of the men to bring the kitchen up to scratch with stainless-steel surfaces and a hand wash basin.

Victor takes a pride in continuing the tradition of getting things done by members and their friends. This isn't possible with the lift. He has regularly to let in the service engineer. For the last few months the service engineer has been talking about new regulations. The alarm in the lift now has to be wired in rather than being battery powered. Victor keeps on repeating that he tests the battery every week, and that the lift is never turned on unless there is someone in the building who can respond to the alarm. Victor feels this additional expense is totally unnecessary. However, at the next visit the engineer says that the lift cannot be used until the alarm is rewired. His visit is on the Friday before Holy Week and there will be activities in the upper hall every day of the following week. Victor tries to find someone who can come in at short notice and do the job – but it needs a specialist and the costs are going to make a hole in the maintenance budget. Reluctantly Victor phones Thomas, the senior pastor. Thomas feels the problem should really be taken to the church business meeting but in view of the urgency he authorizes Victor to get the work done.

As they talk about it later, Winsome tries to remind Victor of all the money he has saved the church on maintenance. But Victor feels that regulation has overruled common sense.

Exploration

Risk is a subject that has spawned considerable academic interest among social scientists. The German sociologist Ulrich Beck (1992) triggered this interest by arguing that we live in a 'risk society', which is preoccupied with low probability but high consequence risks and how they can be controlled. This has resulted in a much higher level of regulation in most spheres of activity with the resulting requirements for registration and inspection. It is argued that the preoccupation with risk now extends to the subjective perception of risk, the way in which risk is communicated and the experience of living in a society that fears the worst. The perverse consequence of the over-use of safety technologies, regulations and warnings is that people can develop a false sense of security and lose a personal sense of responsibility in risky environments.

The voluntary sector, and alongside it churches, have not escaped the increase in regulation and the greater attention to managing risk. Some, such as Gaskin (2007), argue that this is merely a case of formalizing the good sense that has prevailed in well-run organizations in the past. Others, such as Rochester (2001), argue that the 'burdens of inappropriate regulation will continue to stifle initiative, reduce flexibility, restrict opportunities and divert time and energy from operational activities' (Rochester, 2001, p. 78). The delegation of services once provided by the government to voluntary and private organizations has led to the need for regulation and inspection regimes to safeguard the interests of service users and employees and the taxpayers' need for value for money. Many of these regulations, such as those relating to working with children and providing food, have been applied to all organizations whether or not they receive government funding. There have been attempts to ensure that regulation is proportionate to the size of the organization and the risks it is likely to incur. It has proved more difficult to get different government bodies to harmonize their regulatory requirements, so organizations may be subject to a number of inspection regimes (Bolton, 2004). Over the last five years there has been considerable government investment in infrastructure organizations whose task it is to guide voluntary organizations through risk and regulation. There is now a plethora of toolkits and websites and, in most local areas, agencies who will offer advice. Denominations have also made efforts to publish guidance and offer advice on the most significant areas affecting local churches.

The insurance company Zurich (2007) undertook a survey to find out which risks were regarded as most prevalent in the public and voluntary sectors. The following six were regarded as most significant for voluntary organizations, although the report acknowledges the significant diversity of organizations and tasks within the sector:

- partnerships and loss of independence
- partnerships and transfer of risk (usually from public to voluntary organization)
- attracting and retaining trustees
- balancing sources of income
- operational issues – property
- operational issues – public liability.

The term 'risk' is used so extensively that it is difficult to distinguish between different types of risk. In working on issues of compliance in local churches a range of attitudes is evident, as the following three categories illustrate.

Risks to children and vulnerable adults

Given the widespread publicity, law cases and compensation relating to the abuse of children and vulnerable adults in the care of church organizations, there is ready recognition of the importance of this area of regulation. However, there can be resistance to compliance because of the cost and paperwork involved and the time delays that can ensue. For some, the fact that the measures taken do not guarantee safety detracts from their value. Local churches that are part of a denomination or other grouping are likely to be subject to monitoring of the effectiveness of their compliance. They will often provide awareness training to help church members understand why work with children has to be subject to public standards of safeguarding.

Risks resulting from everyday activities

There can be a range of reactions to compliance with the regulation of activities such as the preparing and serving of food and the provision of meeting space, which have been long-standing and largely unproblematic aspects of church life. This is where the blurring between church life and domestic life can make it difficult to establish a culture of compliance. If I don't know what temperature my fridge at home is, why do I have to fill in a form monitoring the temperature of the fridge at church? If I have one chopping board at home that I wash regularly, why do I need to use four different chopping boards at church? If we have been taking children to the park for kick-about football for the last thirty years, why do we now have to do a risk assessment? Risks to people and property can evoke different reactions according to the occupational experience of different members of the church. What seems sensible good practice to one can seem irksome to another. Again denominations can be helpful in sourcing low-cost training, which if held in a spirit of fun and fellowship can even result in a sense of achievement.

Risks resulting from the way in which the church is run

Charities of a certain size are required to show that they have assessed the main risks that might impede them from meeting their charitable objectives and have systems in place to eliminate, minimize or manage that risk.[1] They have to be able to demonstrate that they have identified risks, designed appropriate systems to control the risk, are checking compliance with those systems and then evaluate whether the systems are effective in controlling the risk. These risks can extend to the financial management of the charity, the use of its assets (including its reputation) and its governance. Many local churches will fall under the threshold for this type of risk assessment and many others will leave it in the hands of the few who have care of property and finance. However, where there are members who have the responsibility of trustees, they are also responsible for ensuring that appropriate risk management is in place.

Poffley (2002) helpfully emphasizes that the aim is to manage risk rather than minimize it. A key risk is that voluntary organizations could be so cautious that they fail to meet their objectives. The objectives of some charities include inherently risky activities such as working with people who have been violent or giving children an experience of adventure.

Local churches often underestimate their aggregate voice and should not be afraid to challenge regulation that seems to subvert their purposes. The churches are probably better networked to achieve this sort of mobilization than many other types of local voluntary organization. While the desire for churches to be a place of safety is a valuable one, churches should not be afraid to ask whether compliance with regulation is causing them to shift the focus of activities, albeit in subtle ways. For example, have some children's activities become paid-for childcare rather than opportunities for intergenerational contact and learning?

Those supporting local churches in their efforts at compliance will need to be aware of the different resources at their disposal. Some churches may be rich in expertise and contacts and be able to devise systems easily. Others will be less well off and will need more support, training and encouragement in designing systems and compliance. Denominations can be helpful in signposting local churches to appropriate sources of advice and support, particularly where they do not have the resources to provide the advice themselves.

Resources for reflection

Bible

> The faithful stewards (Matthew 25.14–30)
>
> The care of little ones (Matthew 18.1–7)

In Chapter 4 about money, the parable of the faithful stewards was used to commend the taking of risks in order to put assets to productive use. This chapter talks about risk as well. The risk the stewards took was one that was authorized by the owner of the assets and they took the risk knowing they would be held to account. There are some risks that are to be evaluated rather than eliminated.

This chapter has looked at those who are put at risk without being able to consent. This type of risk is managed by being assessed, appropriate precautions being put in place and monitored, and by those being responsible for managing the risk being held to account. Jesus' evaluation of children was counter-cultural. He saw them as exemplars of the citizens of the Kingdom of heaven. Welcoming a child with the same seriousness that a rabbi would be welcomed was a measure of humility. Jesus issues a warning using a metaphor of real intensity against being the downfall of a child. We know now that the consequences of stumbling blocks placed in front of children can last a lifetime – whatever the form of abuse, neglect or exploitation. The consequences go on to shape the adult life and often the parenting of the next generation.

Harvey (2004, p. 66) argues that the phrase 'little ones'

refers to the weaker and more insignificant members of the Christian fellowship and not necessarily to children. Although the focus of safeguarding efforts is children, there is a growing acceptance that churches contain vulnerable adults whose safety must also be protected. Given this understanding, there is a responsibility for churches to anticipate the ways in which vulnerable people might become prey to human sinfulness and weakness. The church needs to be a safe space for those unable to give full adult consent and those open to manipulation. None of the measures taken can guarantee safety but the intention of safety can be made clear through procedures and training.

Doctrine

Incarnation

Jesus ran the normal risks of life in his time: childbirth, journeys in infancy, learning his trade, living as a Jew in an occupied country. Luke's Gospel emphasizes the choice of his parents and their role in nurturing and protecting him. The doctrine of the incarnation recognizes the scandal of the particularity of Jesus as fully human. God's mission is subject to the contingencies of human existence. The church still struggles with this, often wanting mission to be something that operates on a higher plane, that doesn't have to concern itself with the wiring of lifts. Jesus' inauguration of a Kingdom that seeks the will of the Father is to be realized on earth as well as in heaven.

Walter Lowe shows that throughout history the Christian tradition has struggled to affirm both Christ's divinity and his humanity (Hodgson and King, 2008, ch. 8). There have been tendencies to regard his humanity as miraculous or as passive in relation to his divinity. Lowe points to Schleiermacher as the modern theologian who was most influential in showing that belief in the human nature of Christ entails his 'unreserved participation in finitude and freedom' (Hodgson and King, 2008, p. 238). Jesus 'freely chose and actively embraced' his life course. It is this understanding of the incarnation that paves the way for the approach to practical theology taken in this book.

The incarnation is a sending, and it is also a relationship. The dialogue between Father and Son continues. As an agent of the Kingdom, the church is in relationship with the sending God. This implies a willingness to give an account of our stewardship.

Planning for practice

This section addresses the way in which the different cultural forms of church address risk and suggests further action.

Parish

There will be appointed officers with responsibility for different aspects of risk regulation and accountability, but they may vary greatly in the resources and expertise available to them to manage those responsibilities. Dioceses are likely to be the first port of call for advice and guidance, and again their capacity to provide support will vary. Dioceses will tend to focus on high-impact risks that can affect the reputation of the wider church. This may deflect attention from risks to the viability of the parish and its buildings which are more likely to have an effect on its missional purposes.

Gathered congregation

Smaller gathered congregations are likely to yearn for the era of informality and feel that attention to regulation is formalizing their life in an unhelpful way. Their ability to include people informally in activities and so generate a sense of belonging may feel under threat. In larger gathered congregations there are likely to be multiple committees and officers, and so responsibility can be widely distributed. Larger congregations may find it easier to access expertise. Gathered congregations may belong to denominations who offer advice and guidance but they may also be under little obligation to seek or make use of such advice and guidance. Activities relating to children will probably be an exception.

Small-group church

Because small groups meet mostly in homes, much of the burden of regulation will be lifted from small-group leaders. Where the church uses a meeting space (either hired or owned) for larger gatherings there are likely to be paid staff who will look after the necessary regulations. Implementing safeguarding procedures for children and vulnerable adults in domestic spaces can require additional thought.

Third-place church

The issues of risk and regulation will be largely invisible to those who attend third-place church. It is the responsibility of the venue to deal with these issues, and any responsibilities of the church will be evident to the leaders in the hiring agreement. Attenders will enjoy the protections of other members of the public using the venue.

Where churches seek to run third places, they will need to comply with those regulations that apply to providing events and services to members of the public. Where responsibilities for safeguarding lie, between the venue and the church, will need establishing.

Magnet church

The members of magnet churches are likely to have a high awareness of risk and regulation deriving from their professional lives and their experience as parents. It will be important to them that the church is compliant and that systems are regularly checked for their effectiveness in managing risk. There may be officers with responsibility for various areas of compliance, but the lead is likely to be taken by paid staff who will seek out the relevant training.

Gaskin (2007, p. 3) acknowledges that the language of risk can be intimidating and suggests a way of reframing risk management of volunteers as safekeeping:

Action	Risk management	Safe keeping
Screening volunteers	Exclude undesirable people who may create a liability for the organization.	Be confident that volunteers are caring people who enhance what you do, but watch out for the odd bad apple.
Risk assessment	Scrutinize activities, events, sites and people for things that could go wrong.	Think of everything that could make things go as smoothly and successfully as possible.
Risk management	Take evasive action to prevent harm and exposure of the organization to insurance claims and legal action.	Run the organization in the best possible way for the maximum benefit of everyone involved.

For local churches planning to engage in new activities, the management of risk and compliance with regulation must inevitably be part of testing the feasibility of the new idea. Difficulties in setting up and managing appropriate systems may be one indication that the new activity is beyond the capacity of the church. This may suggest the need for paid staff or the need to work in partnership with another organization that can bring the necessary expertise. It is also worth looking at what advice and support may be available from agencies that support voluntary organizations. Sometimes the reality may be less onerous than feared.

Further reading

Gaskin, K. (2007), *Risk Toolkit: How to Take Care of Risk in Volunteering: A Guide for Organizations*, London: Volunteering England and the Institute for Volunteering Research.

Taylor, J. S. (2007), *Reducing the Risks: A Guide to Trustee Liabilities*, London: NCVO on behalf of The National Hub of Expertise in Governance. www.governancehub.org.uk

Websites

www.churchsafe.org.uk
   The Churches Agency for Safeguarding (CAS) is an ecumenical organization used by denominations and Christian organizations to make effective recruitment decisions through the Criminal Records Bureau (CRB) Disclosure process. CAS also offers advice and consultation on child protection issues and those concerning vulnerable adults.

www.charitycommission.gov.uk/supportingcharities/protection.asp
   Charity Commission guidance on safeguarding.

www.charitycommission.gov.uk/investigations/charrisk.asp
   Charity Commission guidance on risk management.

www.navca.org.uk
   NAVCA is the national voice of local third-sector infrastructure in England. It supports local councils for voluntary action. The website has a directory that enables you to find organizations that offer support in your locality: www.navca.org.uk/liodir

Notes

1 The income threshold for a charity to have its accounts audited is £500,000 a year and that includes a requirement to make a risk management statement. Trustees of smaller charities are encouraged to make a statement as a matter of best practice.

7

Decision-Making

Introduction

Relationships are crucial to all aspects of church life, but in Chapters 7, 8 and 9 the focus shifts to those relationships that facilitate a church's participation in mission.

A common experience for churches seeking to be missional is to realize that they need to make significant decisions. It can come as a surprise that the well-worn routines for day-to-day decision-making are not equal to this task. Thinking about how decisions are made can prevent the derailment of bold plans. After a case study, the Exploration section sets out some of the issues involved in decision-making. Two theological fragments are offered for reflection. The way in which the different cultural forms of church engage in decision-making is proposed. Finally, some further reading is suggested.

Experience

Everlasting Life Community

Kim had joined the Everlasting Life Community when he had moved to Edensvale in connection with his work. It had been rather a sudden move, and he had left family and friends behind, a good two-hour drive away. Driving around his new neighbourhood looking for a church, he had seen lots of cars outside the local school and just followed people in. He was made very welcome and immediately put in contact with

Jane who ran a cell group of professional people like him. He learned that ELC was an offshoot of an Anglican church, but was a cell church that had cell groups meeting across the city. The cell group enabled him to make friends quickly. All the cell groups met in the school every other Sunday. So on the other Sunday he could return to visit his mother who was on her own and relied on him for little household chores. Kim was relieved at this arrangement. At his previous church he had felt slightly guilty and as if he needed to explain himself if he missed a Sunday.

Kim applied himself to his new job and found both success and satisfaction in what he was doing. He sold his flat and bought in Edensvale, settling close to friends from his cell group. He enjoyed having the group round when it was his turn. Then their group grew to a size that meant it was time to split into two smaller groups. Jane took the leadership of one half, and to his surprise the Senior Pastor asked him if he would take on leadership of the cell group. Kim would need to attend a fortnightly cell group leaders' meeting, but it was in an evening and so didn't disrupt his weekend routine. Kim found himself agreeing.

As he got into the task, Kim began to realize the skill with which Jane had turned the notes from the Senior Pastor into the substance of the cell group meeting. The notes were mostly an expansion of his sermons and, while he was a dynamic preacher, Kim found quite a lot of repetition as the basics were reiterated for those new to the church. One cell group meeting, Bob and Kate came fired up by a book they had both been reading. They all agreed to start reading it and the next few weeks flew by as they discussed the chapters of the book. Then Kate asked if it was okay if they looked at another book and Kim agreed. Gradually cell group meetings focused more on the reading and ideas from group members and hardly at all on the notes supplied by the Pastor. Kim kept attending the cell group leaders' meeting, but felt uncomfortable when it came to reporting back on how their group was going. He tended to report on the strong pastoral care in the group and their practical service to neighbours. Kim felt he should say something but he knew this was a bigger issue than not using the right study notes. Could this church accommodate both groups that followed the lead they were given and groups like his who followed their instincts? How would the church make a decision like that?

Exploration

Decision-making is not what it used to be. On the whole, people used to comply with decision-making processes and structures because they accepted the authority upon which they were based. There was a respect for the authority that those who had gone before them had used to steer the organization. Now there is a much greater reluctance to commit to working within a particular basis of authority. This has resulted in democratically run organizations with a democratic deficit. Elections for officer roles go uncontested and there is insufficient debate about policies for it to be worth putting motions to the vote. In hierarchically run organizations, the decisions of superiors will no longer be accepted on the basis that they have gained their position by accepted means, but only if the superior is personally credible or congenial (Western, 2008). The impact of this on local churches is not only the shift from obligation to consumption in motives for attending church (Davie, 2006), but also a shift from participation to consumption in decision-making. There are trends both to let others get on with the running of the organization while consuming its services and also to opt in and out of particular decisions according to personal preference. Given these trends, it is unsurprising that the newer cultural forms of church tend to put decision-making in the hands of a few, leaving the many just to enjoy taking part.

Local churches are the equivalent of 'rare breeds' in the world of farm animals. They have as their espoused method of making decisions, structures and processes that they have inherited from their forebears and that often contain distinctive features that relate to the founding of their tradition. These methods are referred to as polities. What makes them distinctive from secular organizations is that they contain some means of seeking God's will. Sometimes the underlying rationale for these polities has been lost to the conscious mind of those making use of them. In other cases, polities have been discarded in favour of secular management models which key leaders in the church have experienced as effective. The Religious Society of Friends have probably been most successful at maintaining both the understanding and practice of their distinctive model of decision-making by ensuring that learning and practising the method is one of the main obligations of membership.

> On taking your seat, try to achieve quietness of mind and spirit. Try to avoid having subcommittees or conversations just as the meeting is about to begin. Turn inwardly to God, praying that the meeting may be guided in the matters before it and that the clerk may be enabled faithfully to discern and record the mind of the meeting. (*Britain Yearly Meeting of the Religious Society of Friends*, 1995, section 3.09)

As if these factors were not complication enough, the local church is often influenced by the pressures that government is placing on local voluntary organizations to be exemplary in governance and decision-making and to follow best practice. Local churches that take part in the complex world of local policy-making and partnerships may find that their way of making decisions is viewed as inadequate or quaint.

Most local churches manage to make routine decisions in a fairly unproblematic way using custom and practice that has evolved. However, this custom and practice can be substantially disrupted if there is a change of ordained minister, and the new arrival has a different understanding of how the denominational polity works. There is usually a process of mutual adjustment which may contain friction. Local interpretations of polity can break down completely when a church needs to make a big decision. Those who are most active in the church often have most confidence in the way in which routine decisions are made and assume that this will carry the judgement of the wider church in making the big decision. Sometimes big decisions involve churches of more than one polity and it is possible to assume that the other church is 'basically like us'. It can be distressing when substantial work has been done to prepare for a big decision, when conflict breaks out over the legitimacy of the way in which the decision was taken, rather than the substance of the issue.

One of the pieces of wisdom that has been established from long study and practice in the secular world is that good decision-making usually occurs under conditions of accountability (Lipman-Blumen, 2005). To achieve accountability there needs to be a separation of powers between some who steer (or govern) and some who act (executive powers). Accountability comes from a dialogue between the different perspectives on the effectiveness of the organization that this separation of powers brings. Accountability can break down where there is collusion between governance and executive powers. Accountability can break down when people are not able to separate their interests as participants from their duties as either governors or executives. Most polities have the potential for a separation of powers but it is not always obvious and can be difficult to enact.

A particular challenge can be the role of ordained ministers in decision-making. In some polities they both chair the governing body of the church and act as its most senior executive. This can make it difficult to raise questions about the actions of the ordained minister without seeming to challenge his or her authority. It can be difficult for the ordained minister to make proposals for action when they are also chairing the meeting. Circulating papers before a meeting can help separate out feelings about a proposal from feelings about a person. It can be helpful to use a facilitator rather than a chair for a meeting when complex matters are being discussed.

Skills in the processes of working with people can assist

in designing effective decision-making processes. There are books mentioned in the further reading section that offer advice. Training in process skills is a worthwhile investment for those who see their ministry as working alongside those in local churches as they discern their part in God's mission. Nash and Pimlott (2008) point out that there are a range of process skills that can usefully be deployed in ministry. These include group work, facilitation, reflection, vision-building, team work, supervision, conflict resolution, diversity skills and evaluation. It may be possible to bring in trusted outsiders to help make decisions by exercising one or more of these skills. There may be church members who exercise these skills in a secular context and who could be invited to apply them to church meetings. Much can be achieved by conducting meetings in a well-prepared and thoughtful way (Widdicombe, 2000).

Resources for reflection

This section contains two theological fragments. The story of Jesus' encounter with the Canaanite woman and a reflection upon the doctrine of the church, ecclesiology.

Bible

Jesus and the Canaanite woman (Matthew 15.21–8)

This story has many remarkable features. It roots the mission to the Gentiles in the ministry of Jesus. It is a story that can make people uncomfortable because Jesus seems to be acting with less than his customary openness. This may be because it is difficult for us to hear in the story the strength of the barriers the woman was seeking to overcome. Jewish identity depended upon remaining ritually pure and so avoiding any physical contact with Gentiles, the dogs. As a nation of dog-lovers we cannot hear the disgust and fear in that label.

The story also contains three responses that happen repeatedly when people try to make their voices heard.

The first response to the woman's request is silence. This is a powerful rebuff. It is evident through body language whether we have been physically heard, so a failure to respond leaves us speculating about whether what we have said is inappropriate or unwelcome. What is it about this topic of conversation that means it has to be avoided? Saying nothing leaves the doubts in the mind of the person making the request.

The woman accepts the rebuff and goes to find the disciples. If a direct approach doesn't work maybe she needs to go through the gatekeepers. This tactic works. The woman is sufficiently persistent with the disciples that they do bring her to Jesus, if only to tell him to send her away. It is common for those with authority to surround themselves with gatekeepers who decide who gets access to them. This can be a common-sense way of protecting someone from excessive demands. However, if the gatekeepers don't have a clear remit and are not subject to accountability, there is a danger that they abuse their power and cut the person in authority off from the encounters they need to do their work.

The third response was for Jesus to restate the status quo. He acknowledges the woman's call for help and explains why it is not possible for him to meet it. As a Jewish religious leader his reputation depends in part on keeping a distance from Gentiles. It is possible for those in authority to listen and to assume they have dealt with the matter by restating the way things are done around here.

The woman subverts the restatement of the status quo by saying that if she cannot participate in the feast Jesus has inaugurated by sitting at the table, she will gladly eat the scraps under the table like a dog. We don't know if this was a direct challenge to Jesus' table fellowship, which included eating freely with Jewish sinners, but Jesus accepts the challenge and acknowledges her great faith. All effective decision-making structures need the facility to listen and respond to the voice that disagrees.

Doctrine

Ecclesiology

Peter C. Hodgson and Robert C. Williams, reflecting on ecclesiology, say that there has been a temptation to believe both too much and too little about the church (Hodgson and King, 2008, ch. 9). There can be a temptation to see the church as a total institution that encompasses all of our lives and spares us from engagement with the world. There can be the very different temptation to see participation in the church as a matter of personal choice.

A significant tension in ecclesiology has been understanding the relationship between the ideal and the concrete church. At times the church has been portrayed as a sacred reality floating above the messy contingencies of historical reality. Paul Tillich in his *Systematic Theology* describes the relationship as paradoxical (Tillich, 1963). The church is holy in spite of its sinfulness. It is essentially united despite its visible divisions. It is universal despite its existence in particular local churches. It is a community of love despite the estrangements that exist between its members.

The Roman Catholic theologian Nicholas Healy has developed these paradoxes into what he calls a 'practical-prophetic ecclesiology', which

> acknowledges the church's sinfulness and errors, not only when it is obliged to do so by others, but by actively seeking out and bringing to light anti-Christian practices and beliefs and by proposing suitable reforms. . . . It thus provides a way for theological enquiry to focus as much upon the details of Christian ecclesial existence as upon its more general patterns, so that it may help the church pursue its quest of glorifying Jesus Christ in everything it does. (Healy, 2000, p. 185)

A substantial barrier to graceful decision-making in the local church is the confusion between the ideal and the concrete church. One response to difficulties in decision-making is to call for more prayer or suggest that there is a lack of faithfulness. This is to suggest that there is an ideal church that can intervene to rescue the concrete church. Understanding the theological basis of the decision-making processes of our traditions will usually uncover the fact that they contain checks and balances to safeguard against human sinfulness, but that they also exemplify an understanding of how God's voice can be heard. These two need to be held in tension.

When a church faces a major decision, it can be a valuable moment to reflect upon what its tradition says about decision-making and how that can be faithfully incorporated into the processes that will surround this decision. It can be too easy, in the interests of some notion of efficiency, to assume there is one best way of taking decisions and to ignore the polity within which the church is operating.

Planning for practice

Parish

Parish churches will usually belong to a polity that has both roles and processes that have a long history and that are described in canon law. Sometimes the long history has produced an accretion of different methods which are superimposed upon each other. So, for instance, there may be examples of traditional authority possessed by the priest, democratic authority exercised in representative positions and a bureaucratic authority exercised by the diocese. At its best, this can produce checks and balances between the different types of authority. At its worst, it can produce confusion and a local custom and practice that follows the interpretations of the priest and so changes when the priest changes. Where a polity is unclear, it can lead to conflict being understood as interpersonal and not related to the tensions inherent in the different roles people are playing.

Public utilities tend to be hierarchical and bureaucratic with appointed officers carrying day-to-day authority. However, there is the sense that in the background there is some form of democratic mandate for their activities and certainly negotiations with a democratically elected body about the fees they can charge.

The default position in a parish church is to do what the priest says. Where that authority breaks down, the wider church is often drawn into resolving conflict. Achieving a workable separation of powers can be difficult when the polity becomes too focused on the priest.

Gathered congregation

Gathered churches are usually based upon a polity that contains elements of democracy. This may be representative democracy whereby the members elect officers to act on their behalf or it may be participatory democracy in which all members are expected to attend decision-making meetings. The aim of both types of polity is to hear the voice of God through the deliberations of the laity in dialogue with the ordained minister who normally chairs meetings. The separation of powers lies between the ordained minister, who is often itinerant and has a view of the church beyond the local, and the laity or their representatives who are settled and have a passion for that particular place and its people.

This type of polity is vulnerable to the democratic deficit whereby elections are no longer contested, member meetings poorly attended and decisions rarely put to the vote. Where a small group of stalwarts take it in turns to fill the key offices in the church, it can be difficult to maintain legitimacy for their decisions, particularly any non-routine decisions. In the absence of an active democracy among the laity it can be difficult for the ordained minister not to become the focal point of decision-making and for the separation of powers to collapse.

It is worth noting that some gathered churches, such as the Pentecostal church described in Chapter 6, and the Salvation

Army, have a bureaucratic polity but with limited opportunity for the separation of powers. The most senior ordained person is seen as both chairing the governance committee and as the most senior person with executive powers. Any committees that exist are usually formally consultative although they may well be drawn into decision-making. Churches with this polity are vulnerable to the collapse in bureaucratic authority which has beset other bureaucracies whereby only leaders who are seen as authentic and congenial gain support.

Small-group church

Small-group churches may have a 'top-down' bureaucratic polity in which authority flows from the senior minister through the small-group leaders to the members. Or they may have a 'bottom-up' polity whereby small-group leaders request from a central leadership team the support they require. A good proportion of small-group churches have evolved from denominations or continue in membership of a denomination and so may have remains of that denomination's polity in their decision-making. This remnant may be used to create some separation of powers but the main accountability relationship will remain that between senior minister and small-group leaders.

In top-down small-group churches, decision-making in the small groups will largely consist of the leader consulting members about proposed courses of action or seeking to mobilize their support for policies of the church as a whole. Members will be aware that the small-group leader has authority delegated from the senior minister. In bottom-up small groups the style of decision-making will evolve in dialogue between leader and members. The group leader will be valued for his or her ability to advocate the needs and enthusiasms of the group to the wider church.

Third-place church

In the early stages of its development, third-place church is organized by a small group of enthusiasts who work together to identify a way of communicating the gospel that they think will reach people either disillusioned with or untouched by existing forms of church. This group of leaders will reach an arrangement with a venue and use that as a space into which to invite participants. Participants are no more likely to be aware of (or even interested in) the decisions that are taken to make the event happen than would a regular user of the third place. The delegation of so many decisions to the operators of the venue frees the group leaders to concentrate on mission.

However, as the third-place church attracts regular participants, there will be some attempt to form a community and so questions about an appropriate polity start to arise. There may be a move to adopt some form of rule of life, which will have embedded in it prescriptions about how decisions are to be made. There may be a deliberate attempt to keep things fluid and operate the church as a network. In this case individual participants can be consulted but participants are not tied down to any formal role in decision-making. This leaves much of the power and responsibility with the core team. In a network, regulating the levels of participation remains with the participant and so periods of intense involvement may alternate with periods of minimal participation. The core team may seek some form of separation of powers by seeking a mentor or supervisor or affiliation to denominational structures so as to have some opportunity to exercise accountability.

Magnet church

Magnet churches are likely to belong to a denomination or to have leaders who are inheritors of a past denominational polity. In either case, magnet churches tend to emphasize the possibility within the polity for having a team of leaders, usually a mix of paid and unpaid, who have functional responsibilities within the church and report to the most senior paid minister. The leadership team will meet regularly for worship, to co-ordinate activities and to plan for the future. The routine decisions of the leadership team will be widely accepted because of the professional expertise that has led to their appointment and because ordinary participants are glad to have professionals who know what they are doing get on with it. Communication will usually be effective and use multiple media such as websites, notice sheets and emails. Accountability will be between the senior minister and those who report to him or her.

It is in the making of non-routine decisions that any lack of clarity in the polity becomes evident. Some may wish to revert to an inherited denominational polity, others may wish to have open evenings in which all who are affected are consulted but with the final decision remaining with the leadership team. Magnet churches often attract members with a range of church backgrounds and so there may be many influential members who do not have a 'feel' for the inherited polity. Conflict may also arise between those who see the church as a good place to be while they have children or live in that area and those who see the church as the best place for them and one they will not move on from.

In seeking to make big decisions it is advisable to draw upon the help of a skilled outsider in designing a decision-making process that will be seen as appropriate given the polity of the church and will be credible in the eyes of most of those whom the decision will affect. This may involve the design of consultation meetings, questionnaires and presentations to small groups that go beyond the routine decision-making processes. It can be valuable to return to the official guidance on making decisions within your polity and reflect upon how it deals with the separation of powers and how it understands the discernment of God's will.

Further reading

Cameron, H., P. Richter et al. (eds) (2005), *Studying Local Churches: A Handbook*, London: SCM Press. Section on Power by Margaret Harris on pp. 209–21.
This section deals with the use of organizational power in the local church.

Boyd-MacMillan, E. and S. Savage (2008), *Transforming Conflict: Conflict Transformation amongst Senior Church Leaders with Different Theological Stances*, York: Foundation for Church Leadership.
Report on research with senior church leaders with some valuable insights.

Lovell, G. (2000), *Consultancy, Ministry and Mission*, London: Burns & Oates.
A classic guide to the skills of working alongside the local church. Available from www.avecresources.org

Nash, S., J. Pimlott et al. (2008), *Skills for Collaborative Ministry*, London: SPCK.
An introduction to the key skills that can be used to help people work together.

Widdicombe, C. (2000), *Meetings that Work: A Practical Guide to Teamworking in Groups*, Cambridge: Lutterworth.
A guide that provides clarity about why some meetings don't work and guidance on what to do about it. Available from www.avecresources.org

Websites

Chisnall, I., J. Bateman et al. (2007), *Accountability: A RAISE Toolkit*, Guildford, RAISE.
www.raise-networks.org.uk/toolkits/

RAISE (2008), *Governance–RAISE Toolkit*, Guildford, RAISE.
www.raise-networks.org.uk/toolkits/
Both these toolkits are aimed at secular voluntary organizations but they set out useful principles and may help local churches engaging with the voluntary sector.

8

Leadership

Introduction

This chapter looks at the ideas that surround ministry in the local church and that are increasingly discussed under the label of leadership. Following a case study, the context of leadership is explored. Two theological fragments are offered to stimulate reflection. The different types of leadership evident in the five cultural forms of church are discussed. Finally, further reading is suggested.

Experience

St Philip's Parish

Ann has been a regular Mass-goer at St Philip's Parish for the last forty years. She and her husband moved onto the estate when it was newly built, as did many other Catholic families from the inner city. The estate is now pretty run down and not somewhere people bid for as social housing unless they are desperate. There are older people like Ann who have been on the estate all the time and who still think that it is a good place to live.

Until recently, the parish was run by religious who provided daily Mass and were visible in the community. One of them, Father Gerry, had involved Ann in justice and peace work. Five years ago, the Government suddenly started resettling asylum-seekers onto the estate. The local primary school had gone from all white to eight different languages within two years. There were tensions between those who were from the city and wanted to get off the estate and those who had been resettled onto it and wanted to try and settle in a strange country. With Father Gerry's encouragement, Ann took the lead in befriending families at the primary school and running a drop-in for the parents in the parish hall. She had had to remind some of her fellow parishioners that the reason they were in the city was because their grandparents had left Ireland looking for work and to better themselves. So now it was their turn to make newcomers welcome.

The Justice and Peace Group had become more like a committee that organized the work with asylum-seekers. Without really choosing to, Ann took the chair and found she was good at drawing out contributions from people. She had found John, a parishioner who was a retired bookkeeper, Tim, a parishioner's grandson who was a whiz with computers, and Sue, who used to work for social services and so knew which doors to knock on. She surprised herself with what they achieved.

Without a lot of warning it was announced that the religious order was withdrawing from parish work in the diocese. A new priest was appointed, Father Paul, and he warned them from the outset that things would have to change. He would not be able to celebrate Mass as often as the religious had done and there would need to be a proper parish council that worked towards the bishop's pastoral plan.

Three months later, John told Ann he had been approached to sit on the parish council. and felt he couldn't do this and be active in the asylum-seeker work. The next week, Sue said she had agreed to go on the parish council and so would have less time for the group's work. Ann felt that the priorities of the parish were shifting. She worried that the asylum-seeker work would be seen as 'her baby' and she wasn't sure her confidence was equal to that. It felt as if what she and Father Gerry had worked for might crumble. She didn't know who to talk to.

Exploration

The case studies in this book have all been told from the point of view of lay ministers. This is not to minimize the leadership role of ordained ministers, but to highlight the often neglected work of leadership done by people who would not necessarily claim the title. The language of leadership is on the ascendant in society. Business schools and consultancies make a substantial income from selling books on leadership, leadership development courses and coaching to private-sector managers. The Government has invested substantial amounts in setting up Colleges of Leadership for the major public-sector professions.[1] Failures in service provision are usually attributed to the wrong kind of leadership and a new 'super leader' brought in. It is not surprising that the language of leadership has moved into the church and influences the discussion of ministry.[2]

The academic and popular writing about leadership is so vast that it is impossible to summarize.[3] Keith Grint, in *Leadership: Limits and Possibilities*, tries to categorize the writing under four headings:

Leadership as Person: is it WHO 'leaders' are that makes them leaders?
Leadership as Product: is it WHAT 'leaders' achieve that makes them leaders?
Leadership as Position: is it WHERE 'leaders' operate that makes them leaders?
Leadership as Process: is it HOW 'leaders' get things done that makes them leaders?' (Grint, 2005, p. 18)

Each of these categories has relevance for ministry.

Person

There has been a historic emphasis on the character of those coming forward for ministry. Whether the characteristics mentioned in the Pastoral Epistles[4] or more general lists of virtues such as the fruits of the spirit,[5] there has been an emphasis on those in ministry imitating Christ. Character is formed by habits and so there is an emphasis on formation, in acquiring habits of prayer, worship and study that will underpin future ministry (Pritchard, 2007). The biographies of secular leaders tend to identify traits of character and formative experiences but place less emphasis on personal habits as formative of character. A positive aspect of secular leadership is its belief in human capacity for development and the ability of potential leaders to acquire competencies. However, there is considerable disagreement about what the essential competencies are.

Product

Some of the literature on mission sees leaders working for measurable results, other literature speaks of intangible achievements. Stephen Pattison has queried the shift in emphasis from pastoral care to mission in descriptions of ministry, suggesting, 'We need the actuality and reflective opportunities that pastoral care provides if we are to avoid becoming thoughtless institutional entrepreneurs' (2008, p. 9). The secular management literature is strongly focused on results, whether achieved in heroic mode or achieved through empowering others.

Position

Authorized ministry is often accompanied by a position in the life of the local church. This may include oversight of the church or an aspect of its work. Some polities give positions of authority to lay people elected or appointed to serve without their being trained for an authorized ministry. The literature on secular leadership tends to downplay the importance of position and yet most of those held up as examples have significant positions with the backup of staff, budgets and offices. Position can be used to ensure that decisions are informed by the views of all those with a stake in the outcome.

Process

There are a wide range of expectations of the processes used by authorized ministers. In many local churches there has been a loss of confidence in the processes set down in the denominational polity. This has led some to take a more personalized approach and rely upon charisma and influence, something advocated in much of the secular management literature. Simon Western (2008) offers a critique of this approach showing that it can create a conformity to the world-view of the leader which can drift from a more rounded view of the reality that the organization inhabits.

I want to add another two to these four categories from Grint, which apply particularly to leadership in voluntary and community organizations. They are suggested in part by the work of Julia Middleton, leader of Common Purpose, an organization that gets leaders interacting with their communities (Middleton, 2007).

Place: leadership as contextual to where leaders work

In local church ministry, place has a substantial impact on what the minister does. What will be appropriate in one context will not work in another. The skills of reading context are recognized as important in most ministerial training. Even local churches that are not drawing participants from a particular neighbourhood will nevertheless be interested in reading a subculture and locating their ministry within it. Ministers may also seek to identify issues that inhibit the well-being of communities and take on public roles beyond the local church to help address these issues. The choice of issues and roles will be strongly influenced by the needs of that place.

Power: leadership is conditional upon the authority and influence leaders have

The previous chapter looked at the different types of authority in local churches and their relationship to polity. The arrangement of authority will affect the power available to authorized ministers. Lay leaders may secure their power through their access to and influence over authority, particularly when their role has no official status. Arrangements for accountability are important in maintaining a sense of the bounded nature of authority. Identifying how appropriate accountability can be exercised is crucial to the power dimensions of leadership.

There is some writing that tries to look at ministry starting with assumptions drawn from church tradition rather than leadership writing. Steven Croft (2008) argues, drawing upon Anglican tradition, that there are three dimensions to ministry: *diaconal*, exercised in service; *presbyteral*, exercised in ministry of word and sacrament; and *episcopal*, exercised in oversight. No matter what ordained office the minister holds, their work will be a portfolio of these three dimensions, a complexity that needs to be embraced.

Not unique to ministry, but vital to it, is vocation. Most denominations put more effort into discerning ordained rather than lay vocations. Yet stalwarts are vital to the ministry of the church. Without them local churches can become 'hollowed out', with a diminishing core of members looking after an ever more dependent periphery. This is not dissimilar to the experience of religious communities who are finding a growing demand for their work of providing spiritual direction, quiet days and retreats, yet a continuing difficulty in attracting vocations to the permanent religious life that forms the core of their community that attracts tertiaries, associates and visitors (Nygren, Ukeritis et al., 1994).

What is the support needed to sustain ministry? In training work consultants and in my own practice as a work consultant, I have had to reflect what forms of support are appropriate for those in ministry. I encourage those in ministry to consider the following:

- spiritual direction or spiritual friendship
- a critical friend with whom to discuss work or a supervisor or work consultant

- appropriate accountability structures for the work being undertaken
- active monitoring of work/life balance
- personal reflective practices such as journalling or quiet days
- a hinterland of an interest completely detached from work
- an active network of friends
- participation in lifelong learning.

Without a considered network of support, there is the danger that spouses are expected to fulfil many of the above functions and will be delegated the task of maintaining contact with family and friends. There is also a danger of over-reliance on one form of support, generating a difficult transition if that person has to move on.

Full-time ministry can sometimes generate feelings of dependence upon the church and so remove a sense of personal responsibility for sourcing appropriate support. This can lead to feelings of resentment when regional church leaders are unable to supply the level of support needed at times of difficulty due to the numbers of people they are responsible for. Many denominations are putting increasing effort into the periodic review of the work of full-time ministers and this can be helpful in showing up gaps in the support required.

These developments are all to be welcomed but they are rarely extended to lay ministers or to lay people with considerable responsibilities in the local church. I hope the case studies in this book illustrate that these people also have needs for support. For Ann, Father Gerry had been a source of support and empowerment but his unexpected removal left her not knowing who to turn to when the new priest saw things differently.

Resources for reflection

Bible

Mrs Zebedee's question (Matthew 20.20–8)

Jesus heals two blind beggars (Matthew 20.29–34)

Jesus enters Jerusalem (Matthew 21.1–9)

For the church, the ministry of Jesus is an obvious reference point in defining ministry. The last chapter and this one have focused on problems of authority as underpinning current difficulties with decision-making and leadership. The following three incidents in the days leading up to Jesus' death show his authority being both tested and publicly claimed.

Humility: Matthew 20.20–8

Jesus turns the idea of authority on its head by emphasizing service over status. James and John and their mother have mis-read the signs of the Kingdom. Authority is inseparable from humility. It is not that James and John will not go on to make a significant contribution in the life of the church, but that they have misunderstood the basis for their future authority as their status in relation to Jesus. When position seems within our grasp, it is difficult to hear that position is only an opportunity to serve and not a platform from which to receive recognition.

Consent: Matthew 20.29–34

Jesus sets out on the most significant journey of his ministry. He could have been excused overlooking yet another request for healing. The many blind people Jesus healed were reduced to begging by the roadside to support their families. If they are able to see, how will they earn a living? Jesus asks what it is they want him to do. Authority brings the power to do good, but it also draws strength from the consent of those over whom it is exercised. The blind men ask for healing and are empowered to deal with its consequences.

Authority: Matthew 21.1–9

Power becomes authority when it is recognized by those over whom it is exercised. Jesus needs to claim authority publicly over those who have responded to his message. He needs to do so in a way that does not trigger violence in the volatile atmosphere of Jerusalem and so subvert the Kingdom of peace. By entering Jerusalem on a donkey, he communicates a peaceable authority. The crowds recognize him as the one who comes in the name of the Lord. Claiming a peaceable authority requires the courage to subvert the symbols of status that so often surround position.

Doctrine

Ecclesiology

The close relationship between decision-making and leadership means that this chapter returns to the doctrine of the church. Peter C. Hodgson and Robert C. Williams suggest that the four classic marks of the church – one, catholic, holy and apostolic – have been relativized by the impact of modern thought (Hodgson and King, 2008, ch. 9). They argue that the church is a paradoxical reality, both a divine gift and a human institution, both a spiritual and a historic reality.

In a search for unity, there is a tension between appropriate diversity and unproductive division and hostility. In a search for catholicity, there is a tension between holding common beliefs and the need for renewal and reformation in response to the present context. In a search for holiness, there is a tension between being taken up into the life of God and being engaged with the world. Finally, in recognizing the authority of the church as apostolic, there is a tension between the exercise of authority through hierarchy and its exercise through service. Each polity varies in how it manages these tensions.

Leadership is sometimes depicted as a process of resolving tensions and achieving clarity. The paradoxical reality of the church means that ministry can mean helping people to hold two seeming opposites in tension: both united and diverse, catholic and reforming, separate from sin and engaged with the world, ordered and serving. Adjustment in these tensions is likely to come through challenge and dialogue. Discomfort with particular practices in the local church may suggest a balance that needs to be redressed.

Planning for practice

This section looks at the different models of ministry that logically flow from the five cultural forms.

Parish

Taking the model of the public utility, we see that the most important officer is the one authorized to oversee the affairs of the utility in a given territory. This involves dealing with all the population in their need for the particular service. In parish churches the priest who is in charge of the parish carries this responsibility. He or she may not be the only ordained minister in the parish but the office of incumbent or priest-in-charge gives them particular responsibilities for the provision of worship, baptisms, weddings and funerals. They are responsible for connecting the parish to the wider structures of the church. The authorized processes by which this priest works are procedurally rational and, in case of conflict, challenges can be made on the basis of incorrect procedure. Denominations with a parish polity usually have a system of canon law and church courts by which disputes can be resolved. Diocesan officers are often called upon to play a mediating role.

This territorial understanding of church tends to focus leadership on the person with overall responsibility for what happens within the boundaries. That person can choose to delegate authority but they cannot choose what their successor will do. This means that the transition from one priest to another can involve a change in the way in which the polity is enacted, causing anxiety and uncertainty for lay leaders.

Gathered congregation

Taking the model of the voluntary association, gathered congregations are led by officers who are democratically chosen in partnership with an ordained minister who may be either chosen by the congregation or appointed by the denomination. Officer roles are likely to be undertaken by stalwarts who may burn out if there are insufficient people willing to come forward and take their turn at the roles needed to run the church. Judging from student projects, churches with 200 members are likely to have about half of them involved in office-bearing of some sort. In smaller congregations, the holding of multiple offices is not uncommon.

The authorized process by which the congregation works is procedurally rational and there will probably be written codes of discipline and procedure. However, in practice, conflict is likely to be resolved by an appeal to substantive rationality, that is, an understanding of what the situation demands rather than what the rules say (Albrow, 1997). This membership-based understanding of church tends to operate with a dispersed model of leadership. Members are relied upon to hold office and to take part in the committee meetings associated with that office. In churches with insufficient stalwarts, there is a tendency for leadership to be concentrated into a few hands and for the ordained minister to play a much larger role.

Small-group church

In small-group church, the leaders are the overall senior minister and the leaders of small groups. The senior minister will put time and energy into supporting the small-group leaders and ensuring they have training. The skills of a small-group organizer are likely to be recognized as influence and persuasion rather than delegated authority. The key skill for the senior minister is teaching, which is cascaded through the small groups.

Leadership of a small group is demanding in that the group has to be focused on the tasks of worship, witness and service while maintaining a high level of mutual acceptance and support. This often means delivering the culturally desirable mix of being both well organized and informal. The group members have strong bonds but need to be open to receive new members, and, in the case of cell churches, to reach the point where the group divides into two.

Third-place church

Leadership in third-place church tends to be entrepreneurial in style. Once one venue is working successfully there is the tendency to look for new venues or other activities that will enculturate the gospel to the chosen subculture. Leadership is likely to be judged by its authenticity to the genre of the subculture, such as a genuine liking for the music generated by the subculture (Oliver, 2009).

Some subcultures are linked to a particular life stage and so groups may wane as their leaders move onto a new life stage where the subculture is not so absorbing. This lack of longevity may be unproblematic for some but may be viewed as failure by others.

Some third-place churches are started by small groups of people who have a shared affinity with the chosen subculture and a shared story of starting the church. A key issue for this group is its ability to expand as the church expands. An American sociologist invented the phrase 'the tyranny of structurelessness' to describe the difficulties of running an organization that has emerged from a friendship group and so finds it difficult to explain how it makes decisions (Freeman, 1972). Shifting leadership from total informality to a structure is a challenge that is ideally thought through before a new person joins the team. If this thinking is not done the new person can feel as if they are being awkward by constantly asking questions of clarification.

Magnet church

Leadership in magnet churches lies in the hands of professionals who have often received training outside the local church. There is likely to be an ordained minister in overall charge but there may also be a mix of authorized lay ministers and employees supporting the different programmes of the church. Respect for competence is likely to be a key source of authority for leadership but the attraction of personal charisma is also likely to be important. There will be a sense that there is something beyond effective management and professionalism that marks out a good leader. Conflicts will be resolved by interpersonal relationships rather than formal decision-making processes. Informality will be a prized way of working. The exception to this will be the safeguarding of children where documented procedures will be in place and observed.

In exploring the topic of leadership in your local church, it may be helpful to make a list of the different terms that are used and explore both what tasks people with those labels are asked to perform and also what the theological significance of that role is. The six 'p's – person, product, position, process, place and power – can be used to analyse the expectations of a particular role and may create a more rounded job description than a list of tasks to be performed. It is also valuable to encourage the persons undertaking the role to identify the support they need and how they will obtain it.

Further reading

Adair, J. and J. Nelson (eds) (2004), *Creative Church Leadership*, Norwich: Canterbury Press.
A collection of short essays with an appendix that offers a good

guide to the literature and relevant organizations.

Clark, C. and RAISE (2006), *Leadership: A RAISE Toolkit*, Guildford: RAISE.
Available from www.raise-networks.org.uk/toolkits/ A simple toolkit for voluntary organizations.
Croft, S. (2008), *Ministry in Three Dimensions*, London: Darton Longman and Todd.
A model for leadership in Anglican ministry but with wider application.
Potter, P. (2001), *The Challenge of Cell Church: Getting to Grips with Cell Church Values*, Abingdon: Bible Reading Fellowship.
An introduction to cell church from an Anglican ordained minister with experience.
Western, S. (2008), *Leadership: A Critical Text*, London: Sage.
A discussion of existing models of leadership and the case for a new model.

Websites

http://churchleadershipfoundation.org
Foundation for Church Leadership. Publications and research on church leadership.
www.celluk.org.uk
An organization providing resources and support for cell churches.
www.freshexpressions.org.uk
Information about and guidance for those setting up new forms of church, including examples of third-place church.

Notes

1 See, for example, the National College of School Leadership www.ncsl.org.uk and the Leadership Foundation for Higher Education www.lfhe.ac.uk

2 See the Foundation for Church Leadership www.church leadershipfoundation.org

3 S. Croft, *Focus on Leadership*, York, Foundation for Church Leadership, 2005.
This a helpful summary that relates the literature to the Christian tradition.

4 1 Timothy 3.2–5 (NRSV): 'Now a bishop must be above reproach, married only once, temperate, sensible, respectable, hospitable, an apt

teacher, not a drunkard, not violent but gentle, not quarrelsome, and not a lover of money. He must manage his own household well, keeping his children submissive and respectful in every way.'

5 Galatians 5.22–23 (NRSV): 'the fruit of the Spirit is love, joy, peace, patience, kindness, generosity, faithfulness, gentleness, and self-control.'

9

Partnership

Introduction and purpose

Local churches build relationships with their context. This chapter deals with the relationships they form with other organizations. It starts with a case study and then explores the context of forming partnerships for local churches. Two theological fragments are offered and then the implications of forming partnerships for the five cultural forms of church are explored. Further reading and websites are suggested.

Experience

Gladsdale Baptist Church

Gladsdale Baptist Church (GBC) is in a nondescript suburb of a large city. It is not far enough out to be 'desirable', nor is it far enough in to be 'deprived'. It does have a railway station, and a major road into the city centre passes through it making it attractive to commuters. Twenty years ago GBC was in fairly dire straights. Its membership had declined as some members had prospered and moved to outer suburbs, its buildings were in need of repair, and it faced the decision of whether to reduce from a full-time to a part-time minister. It was approached by a woman who wanted to set up a private nursery school and was looking for premises convenient for commuting parents.

An arrangement was made, and the nursery soon developed into a thriving concern. On the strength of that income the building was gradually renovated, with part of it adapted for the nursery and the salary of the minister secured. As the church regained confidence, it put on activities for young children, such as beavers, cubs, rainbows and brownies. The nursery acted as free advertising to the families for these church-run activities. The only disappointment was that so few of these children and their families took part in the worshipping life of the church. Christmas, Mothers' Day and Harvest were popular, but otherwise families were grateful to the church but did not want to get involved.

Twenty years on, the congregation has more grandparents than parents in its membership. Recently, half a dozen members have been drawn into discussions about the need for a drop-in centre for older people in the suburb. It is felt that social services concentrate on the frail elderly and that there is nothing for those who are living alone but still able to care for themselves. A city-wide charity has become involved and confirmed that statutory funding is unlikely to be available. However, it is willing to form a partnership with local organizations that are able to make a commitment by providing money and volunteers. Two other local churches have been involved in these initial discussions.

The members report back to the church meeting. They suggest that GBC should switch its focus from young children to older people, who are more likely to join its congregation. This is an opportunity to be in at the beginning of something new. The treasurer reminds the meeting of how dependent they are on the income from the nursery school. He doesn't want a change of policy that might disrupt that relationship.

Exploration

The word partnership is applied to a wide range of relationships. In the case of Gladsdale Baptist Church there is a proposal that a number of local voluntary organizations, including churches, should form a partnership with a city-wide voluntary organization. Local churches also form relationships with private-sector organizations, such as the nursery, or with public-sector organizations, such as schools. Ecumenical relationships can be formed between churches in a locality to undertake a common task, and in some areas there may also be interfaith relationships between different faith communities. A common experience for churches is to develop relationships as a result of hosting another organization on its premises. But are these different relationships partnerships? This section suggests three dimensions of a relationship that bear scrutiny: politics, policy and practice.

The politics of a relationship can tell you where the power lies. The relationship may be an exchange where each party negotiates and obtains a resource they want. In the case of GBC, the nursery had a need for well-located premises and the church had a need for money. In local churches, the exchange may be a tangible resource for a less tangible resource. If GBC had not needed the money, it might have been willing to let the nursery have use of their premises for a very low rent so that the building was seen to have been of service to the community: the presence of the nursery thus increasing the legitimacy of the church.

However, it is argued that exchanges often develop into dependencies (Guo and Acar, 2005). The treasurer of GBC feels that the church is now dependent upon the nursery. But this may be an interdependency where the nursery feels equally dependent upon the church for affordable premises and knows it would not be a viable business if it had to move elsewhere. In a partnership, the aim is for each partner to be open with the other about the benefits of the relationship so that any interdependency can become a source of security and strength in the relationship.

A partnership will have some means of making policy in a way that all the partners can contribute to. There can be a fear that one partner will dominate policy-making, perhaps because of their expertise or because they are contributing the most resources. This sometimes leads local churches to underestimate the significance of the resources they bring to partnerships, such as premises, volunteers, knowledge of the local community through first-hand experience, and credibility with local residents. There need to be means by which all partners can exercise their voice. This highlights the importance of designing decision-making processes that all partners accept. The importance of designing decision-making structures and processes recommended in Chapter 7 applies equally to partnerships.

A partnership will have spent time reaching agreement on practice. If a service is being provided this will relate to areas such as risk, regulation and accountability. If advocacy or campaigning is involved, it will relate to protocols about who can speak for whom and with what prior agreement. A balance is needed between wanting to specify in advance what good practice is and leaving room for practice to develop and be reviewed. There can be fears that a disagreement over practice will lead to the dissolving of a partnership, but if the approach to reflection advocated in this book is adopted such differences can be triggers for learning. It may also be possible to agree to the same practices from different points of view. So time for patient exploration of differences needs to be built into the partnership relationship.

A key issue in setting up partnerships is to identify what level of formality is appropriate in the relationship. When I did my doctoral research on the social action of the local church, I discovered that there was a whole spectrum of ways in which churches were involved in their communities. They seemed to vary both in the amount of resource they required from the church and the level of formality involved. The box below summarizes my conclusions.

The social action of the local church (taken from Cameron, 1998)

Spectrum	Dimensions informal	low resource
• social integration[1]	↑	↑
• informal pastoral care		
• organized pastoral care		
• mutual aid/ self help groups		↓
• social action projects		high resource
• indirect welfare work (e.g. prison visiting)		↑
• groups of local churches running projects		
• a local church working in partnership with a voluntary agency		
• voluntary agency drawing most of its volunteers from local churches	↓ formal	↓ low resource

It seemed that those churches that were most comfortable with the relationships they formed were those who operated at a level of formality that they had the skills to handle and got involved in activities that they could afford to resource.

Another factor I observed in successful relationships was that there was an agreed way of managing the relationship. The more the partnership took the church into areas with which it was unfamiliar, or which needed a recognized expertise, the more intensive the means of integration between partners needed to be. Organizational theorists Lawrence and Lorsch (1967) came up with a list of these integrating devices over forty years ago. While they had manufacturing companies in mind, I think the list can be adapted to the relationship between a partnership activity and the work of the local church. The more intensive the need for integration, the greater the need to use devices lower down the list.

- Paper systems – for example, a written report exchanging information.
- Managerial hierarchies – for example, the managers of two activities reporting to the same boss.
- Liaison between managers – for example, specific meetings to co-ordinate the work of different activities.
- Cross-function teams – for example, setting up a committee with members from each activity to tackle a common problem.
- Individuals assigned an integrating role – for example, giving a member of one activity responsibility for ensuring the exchange of information between both activities.
- Integrating departments – for cases where smooth integration is vital, a whole department may be set up to ensure it happens.

A frustration I often experience when looking at the social action of local churches is that the lessons learned from providing a service are not translated into advocacy on behalf of individual users or into campaigning for changes in policy that would benefit users. Local social action is often the fine mesh that picks up problems in the safety net of welfare delivered by those the Government pays to deliver a service available to all who need it. This is where joining para-church organizations such as Housing Justice or Church Action on Poverty can help churches translate their everyday experiences into messages that policy-makers can hear. A partnership beyond the local context with an organization with campaigning expertise can help amplify local voices.

A frustration expressed by Ann Morisy (2004), in her book *Journeying Out*, is that the church can be involved in providing meaningful help for body, mind and emotions but fail to open up the possibility of spiritual help or support. Her proposal is that churches should set up chaplaincy arrangements in their community relationships to signal the availability of spiritual support.

A feature of a genuine partnership is that we are changed by the relationship: we understand a perspective different from our own; we gain new insights into a community we thought we knew well; we appreciate that some perennial problems can only be tackled by a variety of organizations collaborating in a sustained way. John Reader, in his book *Blurred Encounters*, uses a metaphor from the French philosopher Jacques Derrida: in a partnership we will be 'eaten', but we can hope to be 'eaten well' (Reader, 2005, p. 3). I understand this to mean being aware of what constitutes our integrity and not being afraid of putting that on the table as a component of the partnership. It will then be clearer when compromises are being made and whether those compromises genuinely further the interests of those the partnership seeks to serve.

Partnerships exist in a wider historical and social context. The social engagement of the local church is by and large an untold story (although see the Introduction in Ballard and Husselbee, 2007, pp. 1–6) and can be traced back to the monasteries and chantries of medieval times. However, an overview of more recent developments that influence today's possibilities would probably start with the high unemployment of the 1970s and 1980s and the work of the Manpower Services Commission who instigated a wide range of employment and training measures to reduce the unemployment register. They offered contracts to the voluntary sector, and many churches and church-related organizations came forward. For some, this involved both very rapid expansion and then equally rapid contraction as government policy moved on. This story is well told in Tony Addy and Duncan Scott's *Fatal Impacts* (1988). It established the fact that a partnership with Government or a government agency would be driven by the priorities of politicians and that these were unlikely to be long-term. Crucial in raising the profile of the social action of churches was the Church of England Report *Faith in the City*,[2] which showed up the gaps in the safety net of the welfare state. This almost oppositional role continued until the advent of New Labour in 1997, which overcame its past ideological objections to working with voluntary organizations and signed a Compact designed to guarantee fair dealing between voluntary and statutory organizations. Faith-based organizations were included in the expanding list of organizations within which Government would partner to regenerate areas of deprivation. Alongside this came a rethinking of poverty as social exclusion and so a recognition of the local organizations that drew people into the life of their community. It was more than the capacity to provide services to people who might not otherwise access mainstream services; it was about providing social capital, the relationships that people could cash in, in time of need. There was also recognition that some of the problems of exclusion, such as school truancy, could only be tackled by groups of local agencies working together, each contributing their perspective and expertise. A further piece in the jigsaw was the response to riots in some northern cities in England in 2001 and a recognition that social cohesion was built by local organizations that were in communication with each other across communities that otherwise lived 'parallel lives' (Dinham, Furbey et al., 2009).

Alongside this policy story there is also a story of growing formalization, reflected in Chapter 6 on risk and regulation. Grants to voluntary organizations in support of their work turned into contracts for specified services, which turned into service-level agreements with specific outcomes that had to be achieved for nominated client groups. The more formal the relationship, the more costly it was to negotiate and so the more time and money an organization needed to be able to invest before the income from the contract started to flow. These transaction costs effectively excluded many small local organizations from bidding for funding, making participation in partnerships even more vital if they were to have a voice. With formalization came professionalization and the need for trustees of charities to have access to ever more specialist advice. Encouraged by the Charity Commission and voluntary-sector infrastructure bodies, this has led to the donating of time for community benefit becoming much more like an unpaid job.

None of this is meant to discourage local churches from forming relationships but to emphasize the need to recognize the cost and time necessary to form effective partnerships.

Resources for reflection

Bible

The overlooked widows (Acts 6.1–6)

A church that agrees to meet material needs is faced with the challenge of behaving fairly and reliably. For the church depicted in Acts, it is the needs of widows that are the first to present themselves. Turning to the *Africa Bible Commentary* (Adeyemo, 2006), and the essay by Mae Alice Reggy-Mamo, the identification of widows as a marginalized group is traced through the Old Testament and acknowledged as a contemporary difficulty in some African cultures. Without enforceable rights to property and her children, widows can be pushed to the edge of family networks and seen as a drain on family resources rather than an asset. This reading of widowhood suggests that a core purpose of the Christian community is to include the overlooked.

In order to behave fairly and reliably someone needs to be given authority over the available resources. It is felt that this task will deflect the apostles from their primary task of preaching, and so a new role is inaugurated. The community discern who will best fill this role and those chosen are authorized by the apostles.

There is a danger here that the coexistence of word and deed that characterized the ministry of Jesus starts to be separated. The proclamation of the word is presented as a more significant task than that of practical service. It is notable that two of those chosen to serve turn out to be gifted preachers.

I am trying not to use the word 'deacon' as that word is used in such a variety of ways across different denominations. Its usage often contains different blends of authority, service and preaching. The variety of usage suggests to me the difficulty of enacting the link between the preaching of the word and the doing of the word.

This passage illustrates a number of the tensions that local churches face when they engage in partnerships. How do word and deed relate to each other and is one more significant than the other in Christian community? Do there need to be authorized ministries that particular individuals are called into? Is it possible in an essentially voluntary community to offer a fair and reliable service to marginalized people?

Doctrine

The Holy Spirit

Where people of good will disagree about partnerships, I want to suggest the work of the Holy Spirit as a possible area of the tradition for exploration. David B. Burrell draws attention to three aspects of the work of the Holy Spirit (Hodgson and King, 2008, ch. 11).

The Spirit is present in creation hovering over the surface of the water (Genesis 1). The Spirit breathes new life into the people of Israel (Ezekiel 37). In working in partnership, do we have a shared understanding of the significance of the created order and the dignity of all people as created in God's image? In the enthusiasm for establishing partnerships, it is possible to ignore those things that seem to come without a price, such as the use of church buildings and the energy of stalwarts. These are resources that can be drawn upon but which do need refurbishing and replenishing.

The Spirit that is present in prophets from Amos to John the Baptist is a Spirit that speaks of justice both in the distribution of resources and in the exercise of power. In forming partnerships, do we have a shared understanding of the demands of justice in this time and this place? Is there someone who is being encouraged to ask the difficult questions and challenge decisions? If in delivering services together we see the world in a new way, who is authorized to communicate this truth to those in power? How proactive will we be in advocacy and campaigning?

The Spirit of Jesus communicates the interdependency of the three Persons of the Trinity. If the aim is to serve a God who is always in relationship, do we agree on whether partnerships should value people as autonomous individuals or as people that are interdependent? While public policy is strongly conscious of the interdependence of the well-being of parents and children, it can put a greater premium on older people living 'independently' and downplay the network of relationships that sustain a feeling of well-being. In forming partnerships, what balance of effort should be put into forming relationships between the partners and what into the substance of the shared task?

Planning for practice

Returning to the five cultural forms of church, this section suggests that each has a different logic when it comes to the forming and sustaining of partnerships. This suggests that exploration of underlying models will be helpful when churches of different types seek to work together. What may be seen as irreconcilable differences or incompatibilities may need more detailed design so that each can retain their own identity and way of working but create a bridge which allows two-way traffic to pass freely in discussing the politics, policy and practice of the partnership.

Parish

In seeing a parish-type church as a public utility, emphasis has been placed upon seeing the priest as the authorized representative of the wider church. In forming partnerships each side tends to push the other to identify a source of authority that can appeal more widely than the local context, the person who connects the local part to the whole. In parish churches, it is almost always the priest who takes on this boundary-spanning role. Priests often have a strong sense of serving the population in the territory within their boundaries and so they have an interest in the residents of that area beyond those who choose to attend Sunday worship. However, if boundary-spanning is done primarily by one person then the partnership can rest on that person's reading of the territory and its needs and where the boundary between the role of the church and the role of the wider community lies. The transition between one priest and the next can be difficult when different readings occur. Diocesan officers frequently have to intervene in the transition. The challenge for parish-type churches is to see whether, if the authority for forming the partnership is focused on the priest, the purpose and legitimacy of the partnership can be more widely understood and owned.

Gathered congregation

The natural response of a gathered congregation modelled on a voluntary association is to form a new committee or task group to manage the partnership relationship. That new group will report into the wider committee structures of the church, who will hopefully exercise appropriate accountability while giving the freedom for the partnership to develop. This model relies upon there being sufficient members with the enthusiasm and skill to form another committee. Their enthusiasm lies in advocating for the partnership and the resources it needs from the congregation. Their skill lies in getting the right balance between accountability and freedom. If they hold too tight a rein then initiative can be thwarted. If they are too permissive then the partnership can lose legitimacy within the wider church membership. For partnerships that involve working with bureaucratically structured organizations this approach can seem frustratingly slow and diffuse to the partners. The language of social capital can be helpful in explaining how the process of bonding the partnership to the local church can ensure it remains an effective bridge into the wider community (Baker and Skinner, 2005).

Small-group church

Small-group church is more likely to supply volunteers to other organizations' projects than form partnerships. If it feels a particular campaign, service or mission is worthy of its support, then it will commend it to all members for their consideration and action. It may sanction a small group of members to engage with the partnership but this will be on the condition that this small group recruits from across the primary small groups and doesn't take energy and focus from those primary small groups. Enthusiasms are encouraged but they are used to mobilize activity beyond the church rather than as goals around which to organize. The advantage of this approach is that the church can be supporting a wide variety of initiatives without entering into formal relationships. This makes is possible to change involvements as new issues come to the attention of members.

Third-place church

Third-place church is often entrepreneurial and so drawn to the new. However, that energy is more likely to be focused on setting up further locations and times for its own core activity or to supplying volunteers to help with other 'start-ups'. Forming partnerships can seem too formal and inflexible. The only exception to this is the 'hosting' arrangement with venues when core members will invest time in building effective relationships that make the venue right for the activity. Sometimes this will involve a contract for facilities provided, on other occasions it may be the informal use of 'downtime' in the venue. Third places are often nodes in people's networks and so the overlapping of networks to multiply connections is encouraged, but these connections are usually between individuals rather than the church as a corporate body. The denser the networks, the more likely someone is to know 'someone who can . . .', that is, a gatekeeper to a needed resource or skill.

Magnet church

Corporate identity is crucial to magnet churches and partnership can threaten the clarity of that identity. A magnet church may be happy to supply resources and people to partnership activities as long as that partnership has an identity at arm's length to its own. New activities and campaigns are often welcomed as signs of vitality and innovation but they are likely to be incorporated into the church as a new department or supported through trusted para-church agencies that bring expertise and have a compatible theology.

My reading of the potential for partnership in these cultural forms is that the parish and gathered congregation are more likely to enter into partnerships than the three newer cultural forms. Partnerships with these newer forms may not be impossible, but they may have to be arm's length.

Suggestions for the design of partnerships

I want to argue that the use of a skilled outsider can be helpful in forming partnerships. An ability to listen to the different partners and help interpret each to the other can be invaluable. An outsider can help explore the possibility that a partnership may or may not be the right way forward. Avoiding a partnership based upon insufficient foundations can leave open the possibility of other types of relationships.

We have seen that there can be a danger for the gatekeepers of the community to be the ones that act as the anchor points for the partnership in the local church. It is worth exploring whether the roles of gatekeeper and boundary-spanner can be separated and held in mutual accountability. Careful consideration of the variety of integrating devices that can be used between partner organizations is vital, as is the willingness to regularly review their effectiveness in maintaining a creative tension between integration and differentiation.

To return to Gladsdale Baptist Church – their contract with the nursery school rescued them at a time of difficulty. This may be why insufficient thought went into designing the relationship. It started and remained as a contract with no forum for sharing politics, policy and practice. And yet around this relationship grew up a whole mission strategy for the church. Only when a change to the mission focus for the church was proposed did the lack of partnership with the nursery become evident.

Further reading

Ballard, P. and L. Husselbee (2007), *Community and Ministry: An Introduction to Community Development in a Christian Context*, London: SPCK.
A helpful guide to the issues involved in the social action of the local church.

Jordan, S. (2005), in Cameron, H., P. Richter et al. (eds) (2005), *Studying Local Churches: A Handbook*, London: SCM Press, pp. 109–20.
Further analysis of the organizational issues facing churches in partnership.

Morisy, A. (2004), *Journeying Out: A New Approach to Christian Mission*, Harrisburg PA: Morehouse and London: Contiuum.
A classic of reflection and advice on the social action of the local church.

Reader, J. (2005), *Blurred Encounters: A Reasoned Practice of Faith*, Vale of Glamorgan: Aureus Publishing.
An exploration of the dilemmas of faith and practice faced by an Anglican priest engaging in community action.

Websites

www.culf.org.uk
Website of the Commission on Urban Life and Faith with the Commission's report and a downloadable Community Value Toolkit to help calculate the contribution the local church makes to its community.

www.faithworks.info
Faithworks is an organization that seeks to empower and inspire Christians and churches to develop their role at the hub of their community.

www.housingjustice.org.uk
Housing Justice is a support and advocacy organization for Christian work with the homeless.

www.church-poverty.org.uk
Church Action on Poverty is a charity that seeks to mobilize churches to work alongside others to overcome poverty in the UK.

Notes

1 Social integration involves noticing when people are absent, enquiring after their health, stopping to talk to people when they are encountered in everyday activities. It is about showing concern rather than acts of care. For those on the margins of a community such displays of concern help incorporate them and give them a sense of normality.

2 Archbishop of Canterbury's Commission on Urban Priority Areas, *Faith in the City: A Call for Action by Church and Nation*, London, Church House Publishing, 1985. The report can be downloaded from the resources page of www.culf.org.uk

Conclusions

This book has been based upon two arguments: first, that local churches can find ways of thinking theologically about change; second, that local churches exist in cultural forms that can be read in the ways in which they use resources to participate in God's mission.

In these conclusions I want to evaluate the five cultural forms upon which the book has been based. I will reiterate their missiological intention and suggest how an unthinking adoption of the cultural form has the potential to subvert the message of the gospel but how the reflective adoption of the cultural form can subvert the un-Christlike aspects of our culture.

Finally, I want to reflect upon how, in a culture dominated by choice, we can find ways of coexisting as different forms of local church.

Evaluating the cultural forms

At this point in the book I am offering my own evaluations based upon teaching, research and dialogue with ministers. I look forward to readers' reactions to them.

Parishes as public utilities

- This cultural form has been depicted as an enculturation of the gospel whereby the local church offers an incarnational presence.

- The missiological intention is to demonstrate God's concern for all humanity by being present in every neighbourhood.
- This cultural form has the potential to subvert the gospel by suggesting that no response to the gospel is required by the people in its territory.
- Parish church has the potential to subvert culture by providing a service free at the point of need and by living in solidarity with those who have no choice but to live in this place.

Gathered congregations as voluntary associations

- This cultural form enculturates the gospel as a fellowship of the Holy Spirit in which together all believers exercise a priestly ministry to their neighbours.
- The missiological intention is to offer an alternative society that is a foretaste of the Kingdom of God and provides a solidarity with which to withstand the pressure of culture to conform.
- This cultural form has the potential to subvert the gospel by gathering together only those who are socially, economically or culturally alike and so keeping the stranger at a distance.
- Gathered congregations have the potential to subvert a culture of individualized consumers by generating bonds of solidarity across socio-economic barriers and supporting all believers on a pathway of vocational discipleship.

Small-group church as book group and party plan

- This cultural form enculturates the gospel in small groups of disciples who seek to learn the way for their lives.
- The missiological intention is to offer a taste of Jesus' table fellowship and intimacy as a bulwark against an anonymous world.
- This cultural form can subvert the gospel by privatizing faith and obscuring its social and political implications. It

can also be subverted by meeting in homes which are read not as places of welcome, but as sites of consumption that segregate people by taste.

- Small-group church has the ability to subvert culture by building immediate and strong support for living the Christian way.

Third-place church as church meeting in secular third places

- This cultural form enculturates the gospel by presenting Christ as friend of all and a companion who is met regularly on life's journey.
- The missiological intention is to build authentic relationships as the foundation upon which any communication of the gospel, in word or deed, can take place.
- This cultural form has the potential to subvert the gospel by linking it to third places that are cool because they can exclude on the basis of location, price or taste.
- Third-place church has the potential to subvert culture by valuing relationships without embedding them in particular institutions or hierarchies and making God-talk possible in places constructed by the market. At its most radical it can create a place for those with no place in society.

Magnet church – church as parental choice

- This cultural form enculturates the gospel by creating safe spaces in which children, young people and families can follow the Christian way.
- Its missiological intention is to value the vocation of parenthood and see it as crucial in building the Kingdom of God.
- This cultural form has the potential to subvert the gospel by excluding those outside the reproductive cycle (for example, single people, those without children, and those whose families have broken down in some way). It also carries the danger that children can become the vehicle for consump-

tion with the church becoming another 'paid for' activity that has to meet expectations of quality. In its magnetism, this form of church can seek to maintain a distance from other forms of church.

- Magnet church can subvert culture by being alongside all forms of parenting and providing a haven from the aggressive consumerism that children experience.

Pastoral reorganization

Most historic denominations have undertaken or continue to undertake a process of pastoral reorganization, whether in an ad hoc or systematic way. Often these processes are undertaken with the aim of making the local church more focused on the mission of God. There can sometimes be resistance from lay ministers who suspect that the real agenda is dealing with the declining number of ordained ministers, the cost of maintaining buildings and the shortage of people to sit on committees. This book has tried to bring together both the debates about mission and also the debates about resources to see if it is possible for them to have a meaningful, if sometimes tense, dialogue.

Some reorganizations are concerned with how groups of local churches relate to each other, either within a particular denomination or in local ecumenical relationships. Here there can be a real difficulty in deciding which other churches are sufficiently 'like us' for it to be possible to co-operate, either in mission or in the sharing of resources. In discussing this I find it helpful to make a distinction between 'shared taste' and 'loving kindness'.

The theologian Janet Martin Soskice has written a book called *The Kindness of God*. To quote:

In Middle English the words 'kind' and 'kin' were the same. To say that Christ is our Kinde Lord is not to say that Christ is tender and gentle, although that may be implied, but to

say that he is kin – our kind. This fact is the rock which is
our salvation. (2007, p. 5)

Her argument is that, in becoming fully human, Christ has
fully identified with us in our humanity – his kindness comes
from recognizing that he is like us. There is a danger that the
judgements we make about social distinctions based upon
taste are so powerful that they do not enable us to recognize
that just as Christ is of one kind with us, so we are of one kind
with our fellow Christians. A basis for co-operation needs to
be built upon opportunities to show loving kindness to one
another rather than jaded tolerance. As the following parable
shows, choice may be inescapable if we are to enculturate the
gospel in a society that equates choice with freedom. However, it may be possible for us to subvert the culture of choice
by maintaining bonds of mutual affection and accountability
with those who are 'of our kind' if not 'to our taste'.

A parable of the mixed economy of mixed leaves

As a child in the 1970s, lettuce was something of a treat. It
only appeared at weekends in the summer, and it was reliably
the same, green and flat leaves that got crispier and lighter in
colour as you got closer to the heart. I grew up in a church
culture of the plated tea where a slice of cucumber was much
less trouble than lettuce.[1]

As a busy working woman, lettuce now poses something
of a dilemma. I know that what I should be serving is dressed
mixed leaves. But I've also watched the documentaries that
show how badly horticultural workers are paid, not to mention the people who wash, sort, mix and pack the leaves into
the convenient plastic bags on sale at the supermarket. Sourcing authentic and ethical leaves has made me explore the
alternatives.

I could drive out to a smallholding in the nearby countryside
where the smallholder leaves freshly cut lettuce of different

varieties at his gate with a suggested price and honesty box next to them. I see how hard he works to make a living out of so little land, and so my honesty sometimes tips over into generosity. I could join the local gardening club and learn to grow my own, but the thought of the time involved and the likelihood I would get roped into committee meetings puts me off. The local authority is promoting the use of allotments. That sounds more social and fun, if I could get a group of friends together to work the allotment with me. I hope they would cover when I was away on business and unable to water and harvest. An expensive but trouble-free option is to drive to the very nice deli that guarantees to source its leaves from local growers. Or I could drive a little further and go the farm shop, more educational for the children to see where their food is grown. In fact we could go with other families and make an outing of it.

At one level, I know that these options represent a different balance of time, money and effort. At another level, I know that it is no longer possible just to serve some mixed leaves at a dinner party. I will need to be ready to give an account of them and by implication an account of myself.[2] Part of me wishes to go back to my childhood when lettuce was green and flat, but part of me knows I have to make a choice. In declaring my choice, I know I run the risk of offending my guests who may have made different choices for different reasons. Is this going to be a moment of minor social embarrassment or will my choices expose fundamental differences that may undermine friendships? How is it that something as simple as choice of lettuce now says so much about me?   •

A mutual future?

For those interested in the future of the local church, there are concerns about whether all five cultural forms I have described can thrive. Some would see the forms as being in competition with each other. The parish and the gathered congregation require a critical mass of loyalty to sustain them and so they can resent other forms that seem to endorse choice. Others feel that, in a plural society, choice is inescapable and so, while you can choose to be loyal, the tide of events is in favour of small-group church, third-place church and magnet church. Others would want to see this mixed economy as a household in which different members make different contributions while living in fellowship.[3]

In this book, I have tried to make the case that all these forms of church can be missional. The quest now is for the grace and kindness for them to exist in mutual accountability.

Notes

1 I hope there will be some readers too young to remember the plated tea, once an essential feature of church social gatherings. Each plate had two sandwiches of different types, half a buttered scone and two pieces of home-made cake. You would 'have what you were given' or negotiate swaps with family and friends. So there was a time before the buffet, which I suspect the women who made plated teas would have seen as unhygienic. Perhaps we've traded cleanliness for choice.

2 Looking at the number of options that involve getting my car out, I realize that it is difficult to have lettuce that is both authentic and green.

3 I would propose market towns as the place in which consciously to develop a mixed economy, as they presently sustain the greatest variety of denominational church practice while experiencing the cultural pulls to new forms.

Appendices

Appendix A

Five cultural forms of church and the case studies that illustrate them

Type of church	Cultural form	Case studies
Parish	Public utility	Ch. 3 All Saints Ch. 8 St Philip's
Gathered congregation	Voluntary Association	Ch. 6 Divine Church of God Ch. 9 Gladsdale Baptist Church
Small-group church	Book groups and party plan	Ch. 7 Everlasting Life Community
Third-place church	Secular third places	Ch. 4 Barnabus Methodist Church
Magnet church	Parental choice of school	Ch. 5 Christchurch

Appendix B

Illustrative Statistics to Chapter 3

- 71 per cent of women in two-parent families with dependent children are in employment.
www.statistics.gov.uk/downloads/theme_labour/Families_July05.pdf

- In research undertaken by Oxford University, more than 80 per cent of the young people saw their grandparents regularly. Almost a third of maternal grandmothers provided regular caretaking, while another 40 per cent did so occasionally.
www.esrcsocietytoday.ac.uk/ESRCInfoCentre/Plain_English_Summaries/LLH/lifecourse/RES-000-22-2283.aspx

- Between January and March 2009, 28 per cent of all men in employment worked over 45 hours a week. The same figure was 36 per cent for self-employed men.
www.statistics.gov.uk/pdfdir/lmsuk0509.pdf, p25

- In 2002, 75 per cent of families were 'couple' families. Therefore 25 per cent were lone families. Taken from 'Families and children in Britain: Findings from the 2002 Families and Children Study (FACS)'.
www.dwp.gov.uk/asd/asd5/summ2003-2004/206summ.pdf

- In 2006, the average commute time was 27 minutes one way (54 minutes per day) (ONS, Labour Force Survey, 2007).
www.racfoundation.org/files/theukcommute.pdf Section 2.2

- In 2005, adults spent on average 34 minutes a day shopping or on shopping appointments.
Table 2.1 www.statistics.gov.uk/articles/nojournal/time_use_2005.pdf

- In 2008, 56 per cent of all UK households had a broadband connection.
  www.statistics.gov.uk/CCI/nugget.asp?ID=8&Pos=1&Col
  Rank=2&Rank=448

- In December 2008, 70 per cent of UK homes were owner-occupied.
  www.communities.gov.uk/publications/corporate/statistics/
  housingstatistics2008

Bibliography

Adair, J. and J. Nelson (eds) (2004), *Creative Church Leadership*, Norwich: Canterbury Press.

Addy, T. and D. Scott (1988), *Fatal Impacts? The MSC and Voluntary Action*, Manchester: William Temple Foundation.

Adeyemo, T. (ed.) (2006), *Africa Bible Commentary: A One-Volume Commentary*, Grand Rapids MI: Zondervan.

Aiken, M., B. Cairns et al. (2008), *Community Ownership and Management of Assets*, York: Joseph Rowntree Foundation.

Albrow, M. (1997), *Do Organizations Have Feelings?*, London: Routledge.

Anheier, H. and J. Kendall (2002), 'Interpersonal Trust and Voluntary Associations: Examining Three Approaches', *British Journal of Sociology* 53 (3), pp. 343–62.

Archbishop of Canterbury's Commission on Urban Priority Areas (1985), *Faith in the City: A Call for Action by Church and Nation*, London: Church House Publishing.

Ashworth, J. and I. Farthing (2007), *Churchgoing in the UK: A Research Report from Tearfund on Church Attendance in the UK*, Teddington: Tearfund.

Baker, C. and H. Skinner (2005), *Telling the Stories: How Churches are Contributing to Social Capital*, Manchester: William Temple Foundation.

Baker, C. R. (2009), *The Hybrid Church in the City: Third Space Thinking*, London: SCM Press.

Ballard, P. and S. Holmes (eds) (2005), *The Bible in Pastoral Practice: Readings in the Place and Function of Scripture in the Church*, London: Darton, Longman and Todd.

Ballard, P. and L. Husselbee (2007), *Community and Ministry: An Introduction to Community Development in a Christian Context*, London: SPCK.

Ballard, P. and J. Pritchard (2006), *Practical Theology in Action:*

Christian Thinking in the Service of Church and Society, second edition, London: SPCK.

Bayes, P. and T. Sledge (2006), *Mission-Shaped Parish: Traditional Church in a Changing Context*, London: Church House Publishing.

Beck, U. (1992), *Risk Society: Towards a New Modernity*, Newbury Park CA: Sage.

Becker, P. E. (1999), *Congregations in Conflict: Cultural Models of Local Religious Life*, Cambridge: Cambridge University Press.

Bevans, S. B. and R. P. Schroeder (2004), *Constants in Context: A Theology of Mission for Today*, Maryknoll NY: Orbis Books.

Boff, L. (1986), *Ecclesiogenesis: The Base Communities Re-invent the Church*, London: Orbis and Collins.

Bolton, M. (2004), *The Impact of Regulation on Voluntary Organizations*, London: NCVO.

Bond, P. (2006), *Open for You: The Church, the Visitor and the Gospel*, Norwich: Canterbury Press.

Bosch, D. J. (1991), *Transforming Mission: Paradigm Shifts in Theology of Mission*, Maryknoll NY: Orbis Books.

Bourdieu, P. (1979, 1984), *Distinction: A Social Critique of the Judgement of Taste*, London: Routledge.

Bourdieu, P. (1998), *Practical Reason: On the Theory of Action*, Stanford CA: Stanford University Press.

Boyd-MacMillan, E. and S. Savage (2008), *Transforming Conflict: Conflict Transformation amongst Senior Church Leaders with Different Theological Stances*, York: Foundation for Church Leadership.

Britain Yearly Meeting of the Religious Society of Friends (1995), *Quaker Faith and Practice*, London: The Britain Yearly Meeting of the Religious Society of Friends.

Brown, C. G. (2001), *The Death of Christian Britain*, London: Routledge.

Bryson, V. (2007), *Gender and the Politics of Time*, Bristol: The Policy Press.

Burke, R. J. and C. L. Cooper (2008), *The Long Work Hours Culture: Causes, Consequences and Choices*, Bingley: Emerald Group Publishing Ltd.

Burridge, R. A. (1998), *John: The People's Bible Commentary*, Oxford: Bible Reading Fellowship.

Cameron, H. (1998), 'The Social Action of the Local Church: Five Congregations in an English City', London School of Economics: unpublished PhD Thesis.

Cameron, H. (2003), 'Church, Community and Change: The Methods of Review used by Congregations in an English Market Town', British and Irish Association for Practical Theology Conference, July 2003, Cardiff.

Cameron, H. (2003), 'The Dynamics of Membership: A Review of Theory, Practice and Policy in the UK', ARNOVA Conference, November 2003, Denver, Colorado.

Cameron, H. (2004), 'What Contribution can Organisational Studies Make to Congregational Studies?', in M. Guest, K. Tusting and L. Woodhead (eds), *Congregational Studies in the UK: Christianity in a Post-Christian Context*, Aldershot: Ashgate, pp. 139–151.

Cameron, H. and M. Marashi (2004), *Form or Substance in the Learning and Skills Sector: Does Organisational Form Affect Learning Outcomes?*, London: Learning and Skills Development Agency.

Chike, C. (2007), *African Christianity in Britain: Diaspora, Doctrines and Dialogue*, Milton Keynes: Author House.

Church Heritage Forum (2004), *Building Faith in our Future*, London: Church House Publishing.

Churches Information for Mission (2001), *Faith in Life*, London: Churches Information for Mission.

Clegg, S., L. Goodey et al. (2008), *UK Giving 2008*, London: CAF and NCVO.

Clutterbuck, R. (2009), *Handing on Christ: The Gift of Christian Doctrine*, London: Epworth Press.

Croft, S. (2005), *Focus on Leadership*, York: Foundation for Church Leadership.

Croft, S. (2008), *Ministry in Three Dimensions*, London: Darton, Longman and Todd.

Croft, S. and I. Mobsby (eds) (2009), *Ancient Faith, Future Mission: Fresh Expressions in the Sacramental Tradition*, Norwich: Canterbury Press.

Davie, G. (2003), 'Patterns of Religion in Western Europe: An Exceptional Case', in R. K. Fenn (ed.), *The Blackwell Companion to Sociology of Religion*, Oxford: Blackwell Publishing, pp. 264–78.

Davie, G. (2006), 'From Obligation to Consumption: Understanding the Patterns of Religion in Northern Europe', in S. Croft (ed.), *The Future of the Parish System: Shaping the Church of England for the Twenty-First Century*, London: Church House Publishing, pp. 33–45.

Dinham, A., R. Furbey et al. (eds) (2009), *Faith in the Public Realm: Controversies, Policies and Practices*, Bristol: The Policy Press.

Drane, J. (2000), *The McDonaldization of the Church: Spirituality,*

Creativity and the Future of the Church, London: Darton, Longman and Todd.

Durran, M. (2003), *The UK Church Fundraising Handbook: A Practical Manual and Directory of Sources*, Norwich: Canterbury Press.

Durran, M. (2005), *Making Church Buildings Work: A Handbook for Managing and Developing Church Buildings for Mission and Ministry*, Norwich: Canterbury Press.

Durran, M. (2006), *Regenerating Local Churches: Mission-Based Strategies for Transformation and Growth*, Norwich: Canterbury Press.

Ecclestone, G. (ed.) (1988), *The Parish Church? Explorations in the Relationship of the Church and the World*, London: Mowbray.

Edson, B. (2006), 'An Exploration into the Missiology of the Emerging Church in the UK through the Narrative of Sanctus1', *International Journal for the Study of the Christian Church* 6 (1), pp. 24–37.

Farnell, R., R. Furbey et al. (2003), *'Faith' in Urban Regeneration? Engaging Faith Communities in Urban Regeneration*, Bristol: The Policy Press.

Fichter, J. F. (1953), 'The Marginal Catholic: An Institutional Approach', *Social Forces* 32 (1), pp. 167–73.

Finneron, D. and A. Dinham (eds) (2002), *Building on Faith: Faith Buildings in Neighbourhood Renewal*, London: Church Urban Fund.

Forrester, D. B. (2008), 'The Communicative Practice of a Humble Church', Inaugural Lecture for the Oxford Centre for Ecclesiology and Practical Theology.

Freeman, J. (1972), 'The Tyranny of Structurelessness', *Berkeley Journal of Sociology* 17 (1), pp. 151–64.

Gaskin, K. (2007), *Risk Toolkit: How to Take Care of Risk in Volunteering: A Guide for Organisations*, London: Volunteering England and the Institute for Volunteering Research.

Gaze, S. (2006), *Mission-Shaped and Rural: Growing Churches in the Countryside*, London: Church House Publishing.

Gibbs, E. and R. Bolger (2006), *Emerging Churches: Creating Christian Community in Postmodern Cultures*, London: SPCK.

Giles, R. (2004), *Re-pitching the Tent: The Definitive Guide to Reordering Your Church*, Norwich: Canterbury Press.

Glendinning, T. and S. Bruce (2006), 'New Ways of Believing or Belonging: Is Religion Giving Way to Spirituality?', *The British Journal of Sociology* 57 (3), pp. 399–414.

Goodchild, P. (2007), *Theology of Money*, London: SCM Press.

Graham, E. (2000), 'Practical Theology as Transforming Practice', in J. Woodward and S. Pattison (eds), *The Blackwell Reader in Pastoral and Practical Theology*, Oxford: Blackwell Publishers, pp. 104–117.

Graham, E. L. (2002), *Transforming Practice: Pastoral Theology in an Age of Uncertainty*, Eugene OR: Wipf and Stock.

Graham, E. L., H. Walton, F. Ward (2005), *Theological Reflection: Methods*, London: SCM Press.

Green, M. (ed.) (2004), *Church without Walls: A Global Examination of Cell Church*, Milton Keynes: Paternoster Press.

Green, R. J. (1997), *Catherine Booth*, Crowborough: Monarch Publications.

Grenier, P. and K. Wright (2006), 'Social Capital in Britain: Exploring the Hall Paradox', *Policy Studies* 27 (1), pp. 27–53.

Grieve, J. (1999), *Fundraising for Churches*, London: SPCK.

Grieve, J., V. Jochum et al. (2007), *Faith in the Community: The Contribution of Faith-Based Organisations to Rural Voluntary Action*, London: NCVO.

Grint, K. (2005), *Leadership: Limits and Possibilities*, Basingstoke: Palgrave Macmillan.

Guo, C. and M. Acar (2005), 'Understanding Collaboration among Nonprofit Organizations: Combining Resource Dependency, Institutional, and Network Perspectives', *Nonprofit and Voluntary Sector Quarterly* 34 (3), pp. 340–61.

Hansen, K. and H. Joshi (2007), *Millennium Cohort Study: Second Survey: A User's Guide to Initial Findings*, London: Institute of Education.

Harvey, A. E. (2004), *A Companion to the New Testament*, Cambridge: Cambridge University Press.

Harvey, D. (2003), 'Cell Church: Its Situation in British Evangelical Culture', *Journal of Contemporary Religion* 18 (1), pp. 95–109.

Hauerwas, S. (2007), *SCM Theological Commentary: Matthew*, London: SCM Press.

Healy, N. M. (2000), *Church, World and the Christian Life: Practical-Prophetic Ecclesiology*, Cambridge: Cambridge University Press.

Hebblethwaite, M. (1993), *Basic is Beautiful: Basic Ecclesial Communities from Third World to First World*, London: Fount.

Heelas, P., L. Woodhead et al. (2005), *The Spiritual Revolution: Why Religion is Giving Way to Spirituality*, Oxford: Blackwell Publishing.

Hervieu-Leger, D. (2000), *Religion as a Chain of Memory*, Cambridge: Polity.

Higton, M. (2008), *SCM Core Text: Christian Doctrine*, London: SCM Press.

Hodgson, P. C. and R. H. King (eds) (2008), *Christian Theology: An Introduction to its Traditions and Tasks*, London: SPCK.

Holgate, D. and R. Starr (2006), *SCM Studyguide to Biblical Hermeneutics*, London: SCM Press.

Hunt, S. (2004), *The Alpha Enterprise: Evangelism in a Post-Christian Era*, Aldershot: Ashgate.

Kolb, D. (1984), *Experiential Learning: Experience as the Source of Learning and Development*, Englewood Cliffs NJ: Prentice-Hall.

Lawrence, P. R. and J. W. Lorsch (1967), 'Differentiation and Integration in Complex Organisations', *Administrative Science Quarterly* 12 (1), pp. 1–47.

Lings, G. (2007), *Encounters on the Edge 34: Cafe Church*, Sheffield: Church Army.

Lipman-Blumen, J. (2005), *The Allure of Toxic Leaders*, Oxford: Oxford University Press.

Long, E. (2003), *Book Clubs: Women and the Uses of Reading in Everyday Life*, Chicago: University of Chicago Press.

Lovell, G. (2000), *Consultancy, Ministry and Mission*, London: Burns and Oates.

Lynch, G. (2005), *Understanding Theology and Popular Culture*, Oxford: Blackwell Publishing.

Marsh, C. (2007), *Theology Goes to the Movies*, Oxford: Oxford University Press.

Middleton, J. (2007), *Beyond Authority: Leadership in a Changing World*, Basingstoke: Palgrave Macmillan.

Mikunda, C. (2004), *Brand Lands, Hot Spots and Cool Spaces: Welcome to the Third Place and Total Marketing Experience*, London: Kogan Page.

Mission and Public Affairs Council (2004), *Mission-Shaped Church: Church Planting and Fresh Expressions of Church in a Changing Context*, London: Church House Publishing.

Morisy, A. (2004), *Journeying Out: A New Approach to Christian Mission*, Harrisburg PA: Morehouse and London: Continuum.

Moser, M. (2006), 'Primary School Choice in a Rural Locale: A "Right, Good, Local" School', British Educational Research Association Annual Conference, University of Warwick, unpublished.

Murray, S. (2000), *Beyond Tithing*, Carlisle: Paternoster Press.

Murray, S. (2008), *Planting Churches: A Framework for Practitioners*, Milton Keynes: Paternoster Press.

Nash, S., J. Pimlott et al. (2008), *Skills for Collaborative Ministry*, London: SPCK.

Nelstrop, L. and M. Percy (eds) (2008), *Evaluating Fresh Expressions: Explorations in Emerging Church*, Norwich: Canterbury Press.

Nichols, G. (2006), 'Research into Sports Volunteers: Reviewing the Questions', *Voluntary Action* 8 (1), pp. 1–11.

Nygren, D. J., M. D. Ukeritis et al. (1994), 'Outstanding Leadership in Nonprofit Organizations: Leadership Competencies in Roman Catholic Religious Orders', *Nonprofit Management and Leadership* 4 (4), pp. 375–91.

Oldenburg, R. (1989), *The Great Good Place: Cafes, Coffee Shops, Bookstores, Bars, Hair Salons and Other Hangouts at the Heart of the Community*, New York: Marlowe and Company.

Oldenburg, R. (ed.) (2001), *Celebrating the Third Place: Inspiring Stories about the 'Great Good Places' at the Heart of Our Communities*, New York: Marlowe and Company.

Oliver, G. (2006), *Holy Bible, Human Bible: Questions Pastoral Practice Must Ask*, London: Darton, Longman and Todd.

Oliver, J. (2009), *Night Vision: Mission to the Club Culture*, Norwich: Canterbury Press.

Pattison, S. (2008), 'Is Pastoral Care Dead in a Mission-led Church?', *Practical Theology* 1 (1), pp. 7–10.

Pattison, S., T. Cooling et al. (2007), *Using the Bible in Christian Ministry: A Workbook*, London: Darton, Longman and Todd.

Poffley, A. (2002), *Financial Stewardship of Charities: Maximising Impact in Times of Uncertainty*, London: Directory of Social Change.

Potter, P. (2001), *The Challenge of Cell Church: Getting to Grips with Cell Church Values*, Abingdon: Bible Reading Fellowship.

Pounds, N. J. G. (2000), *A History of the English Parish*, Cambridge: Cambridge University Press.

Pritchard, J. (2007), *The Life and Work of a Priest*, London: SPCK.

Reader, J. (2005), *Blurred Encounters: A Reasoned Practice of Faith*, Vale of Glamorgan: Aureus Publishing.

Reay, D. (2004), 'Education and Cultural Capital: The Implications of Changing Trends in Education Policies', *Cultural Trends* 13 (2), pp. 73–86.

Rochester, C. (2001), 'Regulation: The Impact on Local Voluntary Action', in M. Harris and C. Rochester (eds), *Voluntary Organisations and Social Policy in Britain: Perspectives on Change and Choice*, Basingstoke: Palgrave, pp. 64–80.

Schreiter, R. J. (1985), *Constructing Local Theologies*, Maryknoll NY: Orbis Books.

Sennett, R. (2006), *The Culture of the New Capitalism*, New Haven: Yale University Press.

Smith, J. H. (2006), 'Mary in the Kitchen, Martha in the Pew: Patterns of Holiness in a Methodist Church', unpublished MPhil Thesis, University of Birmingham.

Snell, K. D. M. (2006), *Parish and Belonging: Community, Identity and Welfare in England and Wales 1700–1950*, Cambridge: Cambridge University Press.

Soskice, J. M. (2007), *The Kindness of God: Metaphor, Gender and Religious Language*, Oxford: Oxford University Press.

Stacey, M. (1960), *Tradition and Change: A Study of Banbury*, Oxford: Oxford University Press.

Stacey, M., E. Batstone et al. (1975), *Power, Persistence and Change: A Second Study of Banbury*, London: Routledge and Kegan Paul.

Staub, D. (2007), *The Culturally Savvy Christian*, San Francisco CA: John Wiley and Sons.

Storr, M. (2003), *Latex and Lingerie: Shopping for Pleasure at Ann Summers*, Oxford: Berg.

Swinton, J. and H. Mowat (2006), *Practical Theology and Qualitative Research*, London: SCM Press.

Tanner, K. (1997), *Theories of Culture: A New Agenda for Theology*, Minneapolis MN: Fortress Press.

Taylor, C. (2007), *The Secular Age*, Cambridge MA: Harvard University Press.

Thompson, J. with S. Pattison et al. (2008), *SCM Studyguide to Theological Reflection*, London: SCM Press.

Tiller, J. A. (1988), 'The Associational Church and Its Communal Mission', in G. Ecclestone (ed.), *The Parish Church*, Oxford: Mowbray, pp. 89–100.

Tillich, P. (1963), *Systematic Theology, Volume 3*, London: Nisbet.

Torry, M. (ed.) (2007), *Regeneration and Renewal: The Church in New and Changing Communities*, Norwich: Canterbury Press.

Turner, J. M. (2002), *John Wesley: The Evangelical Revival and the Rise of Methodism in England*, Peterborough: Epworth Press.

van Gelder, C. (2000), *The Essence of the Church: A Community Created by the Spirit*, Grand Rapids MI: Baker Books.

van Gelder, C. (2007), *The Ministry of the Missional Church*, Grand Rapids MI: Baker Books.

Vanhoozer, K. J., C. A. Anderson et al. (eds) (2007), *Everyday*

Theology: How to Read Cultural Texts and Interpret Trends, Grand Rapids MI: Baker Academic.

Walker, A. (2002), 'Crossing the Restorationist Rubicon: From House Church to New Church', in M. Percy and I. Jones (eds), *Fundamentalism, Church and Society*, London: SPCK, pp. 53–65.

Ward, P. (2008), *Participation and Mediation: A Practical Theology for the Liquid Church*, London: SCM Press.

Warner, R. (2006), 'Pluralism and Voluntarism in the English Religious Economy', *Journal of Contemporary Religion* 21 (3), pp. 389–404.

Western, S. (2008), *Leadership: A Critical Text*, London: Sage.

Widdicombe, C. (2000), *Meetings that Work: A Practical Guide to Teamworking in Groups*, Cambridge: Lutterworth Press.

Wijsen, F., P. Henriot et al. (eds) (2005), *The Pastoral Circle Revisited: A Critical Quest for Truth and Transformation*, Maryknoll NY: Orbis Books.

World Council of Churches Faith and Order (1998), *A Treasure in Earthen Vessels: An Instrument for an Ecumenical Reflection on Hermeneutics*, Geneva: World Council of Churches.

Wright, N. (1997), 'The Nature and Variety of Restorationism and the "House Church" Movement', in S. Hunt, M. Hamilton and T. Walter (eds), *Charismatic Christianity: Sociological Perspectives*, Basingstoke: Macmillan, pp. 60–75.

Wright, T. (2001), *Luke for Everyone*, London: SPCK.

Yeo, S. (1976), *Religion and Voluntary Organisations in Crisis*, London: Croom Helm.

Zurich (2007), *Perception and Reality: The Real Risks for Public Service and Charitable Organisations*, company report.

Index

Bible Quotations

The leading Christian newspaper for less than the price of a coffee!

From the erudite to the everyday, from the inspiring to the irreverent, from the vital to the silly, the *Church Times* keeps you fully informed each week of everything new in the Church and its relationship with the world

For just £65, the *Church Times* will be delivered direct to your door, every week for a year. You will also gain **free access** to all online content and the *Church Times* archive via our website **www.churchtimes.co.uk**